ADVANCE PRAISE

"Ryan has proven to me to have a great understanding of business strategy, execution, and the leadership needed to take advantage of opportunities. I'm confident he will help any leader evaluate their strategy and successfully grow their business."

—Greg Henslee, executive chairman and former CEO of O'Reilly Auto Parts

"Ryan is one of the rare individuals with a true passion for his craft, while still exemplifying leadership, integrity, and caring for others. He has been a thought leader in the NBA for many years and collaborated with the NBA league office on a number of projects that improved the game of basketball. Extremely well respected by his peers, Ryan was a key player in the long-lasting success of the Indiana Pacers. Anybody who wants to accelerate their growth and reach their maximum potential while maintaining a successful work-life balance would benefit from Ryan's thoughts and words."

—Kiki Vandeweghe, former EVP of NBA Global Basketball Operations, head coach of the Denver Nuggets and New Jersey Nets, and general manager of the Nets; 2x NBA All-Star

"Most of us understand the concept of diminishing returns, but often don't think about it in the context of our own productivity. During my time at Lowe's, work requirements were expanding, as was my family. I realized that I need to be more present for my wife and young daughters. I wish I had the benefit of Ryan's thinking at the time, to both help me get to the realization sooner and more effectively reach the needed balance."

—Bob Hull, former CFO of Lowe's; co-CEO and board director of Tailored Brands; audit committee chair and board director of Mattress Firm; former non-executive chairman of SPX Flow

"Ryan and I have had great conversations over the years around leadership, evidence-based processes, and business strategy. He effectively communicates his insights in these areas to help leaders optimize their culture and scalability."

—Josh Wolfe, cofounder and managing partner at Lux Capital

"Today's CEOs need to think about how to manage tough stressful situations and remain full of energy. Additionally, their teams, particularly the younger team members, value balance in their life and great CEOs need to meet their needs as well. Ryan Renteria has a wealth of experience working with CEOs and their teams. Reading his book will help you become a more effective leader."

—John Mahoney, former vice chairman and CFO of Staples; chairman of Burlington Stores

"Ryan's book leverages his experience guiding leaders to help you and your team achieve strong professional growth while reducing stress and burnout."

—Luis Scola, CEO of Pallacanestro Varese; Olympic gold medalist and 4x FIBA AmeriCup MVP for Argentina's basketball team; NBA player for ten seasons

"Ryan's process-oriented approach and diverse experience enables great leadership insights across finance, business, and sports."

—Dmitry Balyasny, managing partner and chief investment officer of Balyasny Asset Management

"Ryan Renteria is an exceptional CEO coach whose years of experience coupled with characteristics of high integrity, intelligence, and passion make this book a must-read for those who wish to learn his thoughtful and rigorous approaches. CEOs and C-Suite executives will benefit from Renteria's years of expertise as a coach that addresses work-life balance and professional business growth while integrating a culture of wellness among their teams."

—Kevin Nagle, chairman and CEO of Sacramento Soccer and Entertainment Holdings; former co-owner of the Sacramento Kings; cofounder and former CEO and vice chairman of Envision Rx Options

"A must-read for any leader who wants to create a thriving workplace culture, with practical insights and strategies for promoting well-being, reducing burnout, and increasing the overall work-life balance of your team. Ryan Renteria's book offers a unique and insightful perspective on leadership, drawing from his extensive experience advising top executives in the Fortune 500 and the NBA, and it showcases his unwavering commitment to integrity, empathy, and excellence."

—Mike Zappert, partner at global alternative asset firm TPG; former partner at Adams Street Partners

"Too often the delicate balance between professional success and personal fulfillment is seen as a choice; you can have one or the other, but not both. In this powerful and thought-provoking book, Ryan reveals a compelling process for optimizing your life and harmonizing professional growth and a fulfilling personal life. I remember Ryan as an extraordinarily sharp and driven investor and was surprised when he told me he was leaving the industry all of those years ago at only thirty years old. Many years later, Ryan returns with a precious gift: a guide through many of the issues that I've wrestled with in my career and life. A must-read for anyone striving to achieve harmony in their work-life dynamic."

—Brandon Haley, founder and CEO at Holocene Advisors; former head of global equities at Citadel

"For the last twenty-five years I've watched Ryan build his life guided by his cultural bylaws. He is a phenomenal example of the results one can achieve with his coaching."

—Dan Levy, former VP at Meta

"Ryan quickly became a big contributor to the Pacers' success through his outstanding work product for the coaches and front office executives. His extensive preparation and deep research abilities were evident early in the interview process and ultimately made him a great analytics advisor. These same skills are clear in this book, and I have no doubt he will successfully help executives accelerate their growth. Having worked with Ryan for nine years, I can say he is a high-character professional who puts his heart and soul into helping others do well."

—Kevin Pritchard, president of basketball operations for the Indiana Pacers, former general manager of the Pacers and Portland Trail Blazers; starter on the 1988 National Championship team at Kansas

"Few things are more important for business leaders than balancing health and family priorities with achieving aspirational growth goals. This book is designed to give leaders a set of tools and lessons to help with that process. I have known Ryan for over twenty years, from when he was an institutional investor in consumer companies. He always asked thoughtful questions that showed how thoroughly he had researched the most relevant topics. I'm confident that Ryan combines this diligence with his vast experience in advising leaders to write a book that will help leaders better optimize professional success with personal fulfillment."

—Tom Hendrickson, former EVP, CFO, and CAO of the Sports Authority; audit committee chair and board director of O'Reilly Auto Parts, Ollies Bargain Outlets, and Snap One

"*Lead without Burnout* introduces a practical and sensible approach to optimizing work-life balance for you and the people that depend on you. Ryan Renteria's unique collection of experiences, ranging from Wall Street to the NBA, lights the path to a more sustainable way of achieving professional and personal success."

—Nick Hartman, partner at Apax Partners; chairman of Nulo Pet Food and Cadence Education

"We all are making tradeoffs all the time, and CEOs and business leaders are making more than most. It is very productive for a leader to have a framework for understanding their choices and alternatives. Ryan has always been a seeker of knowledge and education in all his life choices, whether it was researching investment ideas, breaking down the data of basketball, or seeking solutions to the life choices that executives face. This is a path started thousands of years ago by the Oracle of Delphi when it answered 'know thyself' and pushed forward by Ryan's efforts and thoughts here."

—Ben Bram, CEO and managing member of Watermill Institutional Trading; former managing director and head trader at Goldman Sachs

"Ryan's vision, integrity, and passion for helping others has inspired me for more than two decades. He's expertly balanced intellectual curiosity and wealth generation in his own life, and as I think about the next chapter of my career, I can't imagine a better resource."

—Michael Burke, managing director at Google

"In all the conversations I had with Ryan about basketball, and everything associated with it, the ones I always found myself coming back to were about work-life balance, priorities, and what really drives happiness in life. He brings a unique blend of analytical rigor and emotional intelligence to all those discussions. If you find yourself struggling with those same issues, this book will help you."

—Zach Lowe, senior writer at ESPN

"I first met Ryan in 2002 while he worked on our IPO, and I was immediately impressed by his critical thinking, analysis, and understanding of our business challenges. After that, he made us a better company with his continued deep dive in the business results and thoughtful discussion and questions. Since then, he has continued to demonstrate that insight in a variety of roles, and his insights should be digested by leaders anywhere."

—Jeff Hennion, CEO of Brand Holdings/Knockaround and former EVP, CMO of Dick's Sporting Goods

"I've known Ryan since early in his college days, and he brings the same focus, thoughtfulness, intensity, and determination to everything he does and doesn't settle for anything less than perfection. He knows as well as anyone how important it is to be intentional and thoughtful in managing burnout and reducing stress—and I have no doubt his recipe for hacking these crucial leadership tests will quickly become the gold standard for executives that want to scale their organizations to new heights in the twenty-first century. In short, Ryan can be counted on to deliver."

—Ethan Kurzweil, partner at Bessemer Venture Partners

"Ryan is a special talent and a special person. I had the privilege of first working closely with Ryan when he joined my team at Goldman Sachs fresh out of Stanford. Ryan is sharp, incisive, disciplined, and thorough. His rare combination of critical thinking and positive disposition have earned him much success, much goodwill, and many friends and admirers. After Ryan left Goldman—he never looked back—for a coveted institutional investor role, he succeeded enormously by bringing that same discipline, conviction, and systematic thinking to the investing world. He was one of my smartest clients. Thriving as an investor means taking contrarian positions and having the courage to stand by your conviction. Ryan maintains his confidence through inevitable moments of adversity and comes out on top. Ryan has surprised me so much that...I'm no longer surprised. He walked away from the finance industry on his own terms, pursued a host of interests, started a wonderful family, and launched his second dream career with the Pacers. Then he moved on to helping executives and their teams thrive through Stretch Five, and in the writing of this book, I know he'll win yet again. I'm delighted that in the many years since we worked together, he has been a great friend and partner. He addressed our entire group at Goldman, owning the room with war stories and investing insights and inspiring a group of high achievers to try to follow in his footsteps. And to this day, he's a go-to confidante for his wisdom, charm, and high character."

—Matt Fassler, former chief strategy officer of XPO Logistics and managing director at Goldman Sachs

"From his varied and accomplished careers on Wall Street, the NBA, and the nonprofit world, Ryan has codified his methodologies for leadership success and is sharing them with the world. He's become the CEO whisperer of choice to multibillion-dollar companies, and this book reveals his coaching insights that can benefit any reader looking to improve the quality of their lives, while simultaneously leveling up their careers."

—Jeff Beaver, cofounder and chief strategy officer of Zazzle

"I had the pleasure of getting to know Ryan several years ago working with the Indiana Pacers. I was very impressed with his experience, intelligence, and wisdom. More importantly, I was drawn to his demeanor. Ryan is a humble man with high integrity and an understated sense of humor. I stayed in contact with him after leaving the Pacers because I knew there was a great deal I could still learn from Ryan. Now, anyone can learn from Ryan as he shares his wisdom in *Lead without Burnout: Growth with Less Stress for You and Your Team*. As an executive coach, I witness burnout with many of my clients and I feel it myself. There is *always* something we feel we need to do and there is not enough time in the day. As a result, we are in a reactive mode that leads to stress, which impacts our health and relationships. Don't wait for a wake-up call event. Make the first move and buy Ryan's book. It will help you learn how to develop the work-life balance we all dream about."

—Matt Doherty, 2001 College Basketball Coach of the Year at the University of North Carolina; former head coach of Notre Dame; starter on the 1982 National Championship team with Michael Jordan at UNC; executive coach and author of *Rebound: From Pain to Passion—Leadership Lessons Learned*

"Ryan has had vast experience and personal knowledge coaching leaders to be the best of themselves. His passion for helping is evident in his writing. He has written a book that will help leaders sharpen their skills, enhance their lives, and lead organizations and teams to higher levels. If you only read one leadership book this year, read this one."

—Robert Lorber, PhD, coauthor of *Putting The One Minute Manager To Work* with Ken Blanchard and *Doing What Matters* with Gillette CEO Jim Kilts; CEO of the Lorber Kamai Consulting Group; assistant professor at UC Davis Graduate School of Management

"I feel fortunate that my path has crossed with Ryan a few times, starting with our time together at Goldman Sachs. His high integrity and intellectual curiosity have served him well as he successfully navigated careers focused on profits, then passion, and now purpose. He pours his heart and soul into every project and person he touches and this book will be no different."

—Adrianne Shapira, senior advisor for Eurazeo Brands; former CFO at David Yurman, and managing director at Goldman Sachs

"I've known Ryan since he was a Wall Street analyst and his passion for analytics runs deep. From analyzing public companies to professional basketball players, he has a very unique perspective on human behavior. This book will help anyone who is trying to lead at the highest level with his real-world perspective."

—Keith McCullough, CEO of Hedgeye Risk Management

"As a trusted coach of CEOs and founders, Ryan is uniquely well-positioned to help leaders attempting to scale their businesses without harming their physical and mental health."

—Tom Loverro, general partner at IVP

"Ryan has a lot of relevant expertise advising leaders and puts so much thought and care into his work product. Any leader would benefit from reading his book on achieving professional growth while enhancing personal wellness."

"My time working with Ryan has provided valuable insights and guidance both personally and professionally that I use daily. He consistently challenges me to reflect on my purpose as a husband, father, and the leader of an organization to ensure the proper alignment of time, initiative, and effort. Ryan is one of the most well-read people I know so it is fitting that he now is sharing his knowledge, experience, and perspective with all of us through this book."

"Oprah Winfrey once said, 'The whole point of being alive is to evolve into the complete person you were intended to be.' When I met Ryan seventeen years ago, we were likely on the road to burnout. We were new in our careers and the only thing that seemed to matter was advancing our careers at almost any cost. It has been hugely inspiring to witness Ryan's growth and evolution as an advisor, father, husband, and friend. It's even more inspiring and enriching that he is sharing his insights with others so generously. This book is important for leaders who want to reimagine and reactivate their personal and professional environments."

"Life is always complex and complicated, so prioritizing the urgent, the important, the professional, and the personal is one of the most critical elements, not just in success, but in fulfillment—this book offers valuable insights and tools to optimize that complex algorithm. Throughout life you run into a small handful of people that are so centered, so balanced, and so competent, yet also care so deeply about having an impact and truly helping people. Ryan Renteria is absolutely one of those people."

—Colin McGranahan, global director of research at AB Bernstein

"This is the book we all need, and Ryan is the perfect guide for helping us find that elusive balance between our work and personal lives. In the years I've known him, I've been struck by his humanity, his empathy, and his grace while working in the high-pressure environment of an NBA front office."

—Howard Beck, senior NBA writer for *The Ringer*, former senior writer for *Sports Illustrated* and *Bleacher Report*; writer for the *New York Times* and *Los Angeles Daily News*

"Ryan is a highly experienced and successful CEO coach who has a wealth of knowledge and insights to share. In his new book, he provides a comprehensive guide to business leadership and business acumen through his passion and coaching knowledge. The book is packed with practical advice and insights that can be applied to any business. I highly recommend this book to anyone who is looking to improve their business skills and achieve success."

—John DeBenedetti, CEO of the Corfini Family of Companies; former CEO of Del Monte Meat and Ports Seafood

"Leadership is a lifelong pursuit, and I've seen firsthand the power of coaching and its ability to change how you influence people and outcomes. Ryan's unique experience across finance and sports, combined with his empathy and passion for coaching, gives him a unique ability to bring out the best in people. *Lead without Burnout* is a must-read for anyone looking to level up in all of life's pursuits."

—Tiffany Luck, partner at GGV Capital

"Ryan has an intuitive approach to analyzing managements and companies, which combined with an ability to separate right from wrong, made him one of the strongest investment managers I came across in my thirty-five years on Wall Street. I always enjoyed our conversations as he approached his analysis with a caring compassion unique to many of his compatriots. He served as a great role model for younger (and older) investment analysts and portfolio managers and by putting it in print, he shares his unique analytical talent for others. A must-read."

—Gary Balter, former managing director at Credit Suisse

"Winning sports teams know that evidence-based decisions trump outdated truisms and gut instincts every time. Ryan's new book combines his extensive experience in sports management and executive coaching to offer a compelling guide to success in life and business. He combines sound evidence with engaging stories to show you how to create a culture that attracts and retains the best talent and to optimize your own life for personal and professional success."

—Roger Dooley, author of *Brainfluence* and *Friction*; keynote speaker

"After nearly two decades of working in the front office of the NBA, I've come across so many impressive talents both on and off the court. I can honestly say that Ryan is one of the brightest and most prepared individuals I have ever worked with. He consistently delivered quality work and always had a process in place to ensure success in his area of analytical evaluations of players, teams, and overall trends in the highest level of basketball. His impact on the Pacers' success was invaluable, and I have no doubt that this book will provide people with the tools and advice to help them maximize their professional growth. Combine his skills and experience with his integrity and caring for others, and you are going to have a book that really impacts people in a positive way."

—Chad Buchanan, general manager of the Indiana Pacers

"Ryan has a unique skill set. He is analytical with data, statistics, and numbers, which drive businesses. At the same time, he understands the importance of culture and a positive workplace that adds to a balanced life. This book is a pathway to a fulfilling life at home and work, giving you the tools to answer some of life's toughest decisions."

—Blake Vann, CEO at Vann Brothers Companies

"Ryan Renteria is the perfect person to deliver a rigorously developed and tested, deeply researched, practical, and achievable framework to improve the lives of high-functioning leaders and the people who depend on them: family, employees, customers, community, and shareholders. Ryan has lived a life of focus and purpose with exceptionally high achievement in three distinct areas of leadership: investing, professional sports, and executive coaching. He has walked the walk in his own life, recognizing when his absolute focus in one area (work) was costing him in other areas (health and a fullness of life.) He has been an inspiration to me and many others for decades as he achieves his own goals and dreams, striving to maximize what matters to him and those around them rather than striving to "compete" with the status or yardage markers of others. This has led to Ryan gaining the trust of many of the highest-achieving people across a myriad of industries, geographies, and life stages—and deeply impacting how many of them set and approach their own professional goals."

—Mike Dudas, founder and general partner of 6th Man Ventures, cofounder and chairman of Links Golf Club, founder and former CEO of the Block

"*Lead without Burnout* is a game-changing book that provides a road map for leaders to achieve growth without the stress and exhaustion that often come with success. Ryan Renteria's unparalleled experience as a coach to top CEOs shines through in his practical and actionable advice, making this book a valuable resource for anyone looking to create more balance."

—Chris Roberts, partner at L Catterton

"Ryan's thorough research process, commitment to the highest-quality work, and ability to communicate clearly ensured his quick rise in the finance industry. He applied the same rigorous process to become one of the best at helping executives take their growth to even higher levels, and that comes through in this book. In knowing Ryan for seventeen years, I hold him in the highest regard in trustworthiness, thoughtfulness, and passion to help others succeed."

—Rick Singh, portfolio manager at J.P. Morgan Asset Management; former partner/managing director at Karsch Capital, 3G Capital and Standard Pacific

"If you are a leader of an organization in your business life, you will want to read this book. We all want to balance our work and family life. This book will help you experience wellness and get more positive aspects out of work, relaxation, and family time. I have known Ryan for well over a decade and he has the ultimate experience about his writings. He has been at the highest of his profession and advised leaders in many industries. I believe this book can help change your approach to life to live in a much happier way."

—Kenneth Young, president and owner of several Minor League Baseball teams; Baseball America's Minor League Executive of the Year; president of Ovations Food Services

"What separates this book from others in this genre is the immediate applicability of the ideas. My life has changed for the better because his transformative ideas are so easy to adopt. Ryan is an incredible executive coach, and this book reflects that same excellence in every chapter!"

—Lokesh Sikaria, founder and managing partner of Moneta Ventures; former CEO of Sparta Consulting and Rapidigm

"Ryan's world-class career spanning Wall Street, the NBA, nonprofits, and coaching makes him uniquely qualified to provide insights into achieving consistently high performance, doing so with high integrity, and balancing all of this with quality of life. Both experienced and aspiring leaders in any field will benefit from the wisdom he shares in *Lead without Burnout*."

—Jose Torres, founder and chief investment officer of Lokoya Capital Management; former partner at the Cypress Funds

"A leader would benefit from reading this book because it can help them understand the importance of promoting a healthy and positive work environment, resulting in increased productivity, employee satisfaction, and overall success of the organization. Ryan is a valuable asset to any organization with lengthy experience advising and studying leaders, a meticulous approach, a determined commitment to high ethical standards, and a dedication to helping others succeed."

—Jack Crawford, founding GP of Impact Venture Capital; Kauffman Fellow; former VC portfolio manager at Oracle

"Work-life balance is one of the hardest things to do in professional sports, but finding the right balance keeps you happy to do the job year after year. Ryan came to me years ago with a grounded and thoughtful approach to helping an NBA front office/coaching staff. He listens to what they need and can propose good ways forward."

—Dean Oliver, PhD, former assistant coach of the Washington Wizards; author of *Basketball on Paper*; former VP of data science at TruMedia; and director at ESPN, the Sacramento Kings, and Denver Nuggets

"From working on our IPO in 2002 to becoming a shareholder, Ryan challenged us with insightful questions around our strategy and growth initiatives. His guidance will help leaders aiming to grow their business and create a culture of well-being."

—Ed Stack, executive chairman and former CEO of Dick's Sporting Goods

"Ryan was one of my most trusted advisors when I coached the Pacers. I valued his input on strategy tremendously as it was clear how much preparation went into his work. With his meticulous approach and extensive experience advising leaders, I know his book will help leaders striving for professional growth without burning out."

—Frank Vogel, head coach of the Phoenix Suns, head coach of the Los Angeles Lakers 2020 Championship Team; former head coach of the Indiana Pacers and Orlando Magic

"Ryan always challenged our executive team with tough questions that demonstrated his level of preparation and knowledge of strategy and leadership. Having known him for over twenty years, I'm not surprised he has been a trusted advisor to leaders from the C-Suite to the NBA. I know he will help leaders seeking to improve their business strategy and growth while prioritizing well-being."

—Ron Sargent, former chairman and CEO of Staples; board director of Wells Fargo and Kroger

"Early in the interview stage I already knew Ryan was going to add significant value to the Pacers. I was impressed by how well he fielded questions on the spot from myself and the executive team about an array of players and concepts. In his early stages of growing our analytics efforts, I read all his analyses and enjoyed the unique insights and clear communication. I'm confident he'll be quite successful using his skill set, passion, and integrity to help executives take their growth to new heights."

—Herb Simon, owner of the Indiana Pacers; chairman emeritus, cofounder and former CEO of Simon Property Group

"Today more than ever, leaders need the right tools to grow their businesses without burning out themselves or their talented team members. Ryan's substantial experience working with CEOs and his thoughtful approach to his work should prove beneficial to business leaders who read this book."

—Ron Boire, former CEO of Barnes & Noble, Sears Canada, and Brookstone, president at Sony, Toys R Us and Sears, and EVP at Best Buy; partner at Valize and principal at the Upland Group

LEAD
WITHOUT
BURNOUT

LEAD
WITHOUT
BURNOUT

Growth with Less Stress
for You and Your Team

Ryan Renteria

 STRETCH FIVE

Lead without Burnout:
Growth with Less Stress for You and Your Team
© 2024, Ryan Renteria. All rights reserved.

Published by Stretch Five, Carmichael, California
Publication managed by AuthorImprints.com

ISBN 979-8-9891307-2-6 (hardcover)
ISBN 979-8-9891307-1-9 (paperback)
ISBN 979-8-9891307-0-2 (eBook)
Library of Congress Control Number: 2023918452

TheStretchFive.com

For my wife A.R., son R.R., daughter L.R., mom J.P., and H.P. Creating a lot of cherished time and precious memories with you is why I aim to lead without burnout.

CONTENTS

Foreword i

Introduction 1
- My Burnout, What I Learned from It, and Why I Can
  Help You. 5
- Full Disclosure 7

Chapter 1: What Matters?. 11
- Regret Me Not 14
- How Much Does Money Drive Happiness? 16
- Find Out What You Want Most. 18
- Calm Your Guilt 22

Chapter 2: Cultural Bylaws 25
- The Reasons Mission Statements Have Largely Failed 27
- Why?. 28
- What? 31
- How?. 33
- Lessons Learned 35
- Rank Your Priorities and Constituents 38
- Getting Everyone to Buy into Your Cultural Bylaws. 41
- Cultural Bylaws in Action. 45

Chapter 3: Trust. 47
- The Opportunity Cost of Staying in the Weeds. 48
- My Entanglement 49

- Creating an Optimized Culture. 50
- Team Chemistry 59

Chapter 4: Candor 63
- Set the Tone 64
- Creating High Candor in Group Meetings. 66
- Choose Open-Ended Questions over Definitive
  Statements 70
- What about the Gorilla in the Room?. 71
- Giving Feedback 73
- Ask for Feedback on Your Performance. 75

Chapter 5: Mental Health. 79
- Caring. 84
- Empathy 87
- Recognition. 89
- Thank You 91
- Demeanor 92
- Offer Enhanced Mental Health Benefits 96
- Mental Health Practices to Encourage and Support 100
- Your Goal 103

Chapter 6: Hiring. 105
- Stack the Deck 107
- Traits to Prioritize. 110
- Enhanced Job Descriptions 111
- Considering the Candidates 113
- Massive Due Diligence in Interviews 115
- Checking with References. 120
- Sell Them on You 122
- Celebrate New Hires. 123

Chapter 7: Optimizing Time 125
- Finding Focus with the 80/20 Rule. 126
- The Surprising, Undeniable Power of Snapshots 133
- Ruthless Prioritization of Your Calendar 140

Chapter 8: Decision-Making 149

- Checklists 150
- Premortems. 151
- Mastering Cognitive Biases. 156
- Leave the Office 163
- Elevate Everyone's Decision-Making 164

Conclusion. 165

Notes. 169

Acknowledgements 175

About the Author 177

FOREWORD

"**S**o you're telling me that Ryan comfortably retired from his hedge fund career at the age of thirty to focus exclusively on volunteering. He then taught himself how to code so he could develop his own 'Moneyball' algorithms for the NBA, and had a successful nine years as a trusted advisor to the Indiana Pacers. After that, he launched an advisory firm where he coaches CEOs of multibillion-dollar companies and other business leaders. What's the catch?"

Those were my thoughts when Bob Lorber first told me about Ryan Renteria. I imagine my face conveyed the mix of admiration and skepticism that I was processing. But, having known and worked with Bob for years, I trusted him. Bob is a leadership legend himself: a university professor, coauthor with the likes of Ken Blanchard, and longtime coach to CEOs of multibillion-dollar organizations. Looking back, I thank God that I said yes to Bob and met with Ryan.

To be clear, if you're looking for typical self-help advice or an academic review of business leadership, you have the wrong book. In my humble opinion, there are already too many of those. As the CEO of a gritty, family-owned manufacturing business that employs over a thousand people, I have neither the time nor the patience to read them. Instead, Ryan has used his unique and experienced view of modern leadership to write a book with real stories and proven strategies to help with what matters most, professionally and personally.

More specifically, Ryan shares his knowledge on how to optimize your energy to scale your business and serve as an exemplary leader without sacrificing your role as a parent, partner, friend, and human. This book provides actionable steps to take on everything from:

- A process for honing in on what parts of your life (family, work, charitable, friendships, etc.) matter most to you, and how to address those areas while growing your skills, your team, and your business.
- A process to identify, attract, interview, and motivate "A" players, who can assume responsibilities from your overbooked schedule. This is key to giving you the mental space for more strategic thinking and regular downtime.
- How to create an irresistible values-based culture that puts mental health front and center, improves engagement, and ultimately increases profitability.
- Modern-day, analytical decision-making and productivity-improving processes derived from the ancient philosophies of stoicism.

Ryan knows I'm not one for flattery, but I was honored when he asked me to write his foreword. In the three short years that Ryan has been my CEO coach, he has helped me immensely and I feel fortunate to be working with him.

Yes, Ryan is brilliant. Yes, he has the real-world experience of three very successful careers under his belt. Yes, he is the most well-read person I have ever met and is the closest thing I know to ChatGPT with a pulse. But what really sets Ryan apart is his integrity and his heart. He genuinely cares about helping leaders in their search for balance, so they can drive positive change in their organizations without burning out or sacrificing their personal relationships along the way. Enjoy, and good luck in your pursuit!

—Trenton Mayol, CEO and president of Pacific Southwest Container, formerly at Andreesen Horowitz

INTRODUCTION

"Everyone's health generally declines with time, and sooner or later we all die, so the question we all must answer is how to make the most of our finite time on earth. Put that way, it sounds like a lofty, philosophical question—but that's not how I see it. I'm trained as an engineer and made my fortune on the strength of my analytical skills, so I see this question as an optimization problem: how to maximize fulfillment while minimizing waste."

—Bill Perkins, author of *Die with Zero*

I f one of your closest family members or friends were diagnosed with a potentially terminal disease or suffered a nearly fatal accident, which regrets would strike you the hardest?

This troubling awakening happened to two of my CEO coaching clients. Both individuals were already keenly aware of the importance of balancing their professional success with personal fulfillment. They were empathetic spouses and supportive parents, and took their physical and mental health seriously.

Yet, these people still logged long hours in the office and on the road. Even when they were home, they constantly checked emails, texts, and direct messages. This made it harder to be entirely present with their families and distracted them from fully enjoying their nonwork time. They also had nearly constant battles with insomnia and sometimes had a short fuse when communicating with the people they cared about most. Despite their awareness of the potential for anxiety from work to diminish the quality of their personal lives, they still struggled to manage it.

During the same week, one of them had a sister diagnosed with breast cancer, while the other had a son involved in a severe car accident. Both clients were devastated. Suddenly, the need to prioritize a more effective balance between life and work became abundantly clear for both of them.

At the same time, neither of my clients wanted their professional growth to suffer. Nor did they want to sacrifice their aspirations for growing the business. After all, many team members who worked extremely hard for them were counting on leadership's ability to deliver solid financial results and growth opportunities.

As leaders, my clients felt a responsibility to serve their companies' best interests and secure a prosperous financial future for all stakeholders. As spouses, parents, friends, community members, and humans, they felt the need to be more available.

Does any of this sound relatable?

Perhaps your perfectionism, ambition, or guilt about how hard you think you must work puts a strain on your relationships, hurts your mental or physical health, or makes a high quality of life difficult to achieve. You might also be under tremendous pressure to make critical decisions almost daily, causing you to feel isolated without many outlets for help.

Is it possible to be a great leader and be personally fulfilled in the ways that matter most to you?

Unequivocally, the answer is yes. You just need the skills and tools to make it happen.

The key to work-life optimization and burnout elimination is to create a world-class culture of well-being with best practices for attracting "A" players. Entrust these talented team members with more ownership over some of your responsibilities and they will be motivated to take them off your plate. Optimize productivity and decision-making to free up more time and mental energy for everyone.

This book will explain this road map to optimize your professional and personal growth. More specifically, think of the following as an executive summary of the benefits you will get from reading it.

- Chapter 1 will show you how true self-actualization stems from rating highly in many, but not all, aspects of personal and professional life.
- Chapter 2 will teach you how to create cultural bylaws that will help you better attract and retain talent as well as make more informed decisions.
- Chapter 3 is about establishing a culture of two-way trust that frees up your time for strategic thinking, gives your team members greater purpose, and enhances talent retention.
- Chapter 4 outlines how to create a culture of high candor that improves learning, decision quality, and employee engagement.
- Chapter 5 is about unique ways to prioritize mental health in your workplace culture. It is part of a socially responsible leadership style that sends loyalty through the roof.
- Chapter 6 gives you the step-by-step process for top-notch due diligence to land "A" players that radically improve your life.

- Chapter 7 lays out the strategies to optimize your time and productivity, including a unique application of the 80/20 Principle, snapshots, and calendar analysis.
- Chapter 8 centers on improving decision-making through lessons checklists, premortems, and mastery of cognitive biases.

Each of these chapters includes parts of an evidence-based process that will optimize professional success with personal wellness for you and your team. The ideas presented will also enable you to grow your business more effectively than you ever would with stress and anxiety contributing to burnout.

So, what happened to the clients mentioned in the opening?

For starters, they were eternally grateful to get a second chance. The first client's sister completely beat breast cancer and remains cancer-free today. The second person's son fully recovered from the car accident without any permanent damage.

A sigh of relief followed, but these people were too smart to dismiss the incidents without taking action. With the skills and actionable tools presented in the chapters ahead, they have made significant strides in optimizing their work and personal lives.

Today, they spend fewer hours in the office and on the road. They sleep better and are far more present at home. Yet, none of this personal growth has affected their ability to scale their businesses. One of them is well on their way to leading their company to $1.5 billion in revenues at higher margins. The other has taken their 30 percent annual investment returns to even higher levels while expanding into several brand-new areas.

Perhaps most importantly, both clients put even more emphasis on mental health and wellness as top priorities in their workplace culture, broadening counseling and wellness offerings, making fitness more accessible, and expanding professional development. This has helped their team members by giving them the tools they need to maximize their own professional and personal lives, as evidenced by heartfelt employee feedback and external recognition. It has also provided my clients with a sense of positive impact on the lives of others.

MY BURNOUT, WHAT I LEARNED FROM IT, AND WHY I CAN HELP YOU

I've spent twenty-two years studying and advising leaders. My first career was on Wall Street, primarily working for two hedge funds where I decided which CEOs and companies to back with investments. Although I am eternally grateful for all the opportunities I had and the brilliant people I met in that business, the toll it took on my physical and mental health was unsustainable. My anxiety and stress levels were off the charts; I ate poorly, had almost no time for exercise, and rarely slept for more than four hours without interruption.

If you applied a rating to my work life, it might have been close to a ten out of ten. I was intellectually stimulated, working with incredibly talented people, and able to contribute to the firm's strong performance. I was blessed with an environment where I attained the financial independence to choose any path in life I wanted going forward. If you were to rate my life away from work, however, it was probably a one out of ten. The net result was a burnt-out me.

I decided to leave the hedge fund business at thirty years old. My next step likely would have been to start my own investment firm, but I walked away from it all. Why? I felt it would have destroyed everything else that mattered to me, because I hadn't yet obtained all the lessons in work-life optimization and leadership that I have today.

For the next two years, my only career was volunteering for charitable organizations. I spent time volunteering at local children's hospitals, the Ronald McDonald House, the Make-A-Wish

Foundation, the Special Olympics, and the Manhattan Child Advocacy Center. All of these experiences were highly rewarding, but they still weren't the answer to what I was looking for. Did I even know what I was looking for? At that point, probably not.

There was a deep void inside me. I loved volunteering, and I enjoyed the free time I had to be with my family and do things for my own wellness. But I missed having a career. I needed something to challenge me intellectually.

All work, all the time was no way to live, but neither was having zero professional life. I needed to find a way to get the most out of what I liked about each aspect of my life.

I had always loved basketball and had a background in predictive modeling and statistical analysis from Wall Street. When the Indiana Pacers owner hired me as a basketball analytics advisor to the front office executives and coaches, I jumped at the chance to re-enter the professional world in such a fun role. I also felt lucky for the opportunity to join a successful franchise that is considered one of the classiest in the league, due to the culture created by the Simon family and fostered by their executives.

I had nine years of amazing experiences with the Pacers, from being in our war room on NBA draft night to learning many valuable lessons about leadership and culture from the organization. But I chose not to pursue more all-consuming opportunities because I had not yet put together the necessary skills to balance such intense roles with my desire to be fully present for my family.

My interest in leadership and professional development was growing immensely. I served on the advisory board of The Private Placement Group, an executive recruitment and placement agency in the financial services industry. On Wednesday evenings for eight years, I provided pro bono career coaching sessions through the New York Science, Industry, and Business Library. This led to me coaching executives, honing the framework outlined in this book, and starting Stretch Five, where I coach CEOs and business leaders to optimize their professional and personal performance and growth. I work with a dozen high-performing CEOs in a group setting and many in one-on-one sessions. I help them reduce overload and overcome challenges to achieve new levels of impact and connection with their businesses and families.

Finally, I had my answer to what I was looking for—neither extreme is viable. I did not want my career to be *all* of me, but I needed it to be a big part of me.

My career has been a dynamic, challenging, and enlightening experience, and I wouldn't change any of it. Although each decision I made was the right one for me, I mistakenly assumed those leadership roles would destroy most nonprofessional areas of my life. At those points in my career, I had not yet realized that I could excel as a leader *and* have a happy, fulfilling life while helping others around me to also grow.

It is only after years of research and experience as a CEO coach that I've learned and developed a process for optimizing professional growth while maintaining a healthy, balanced personal life. Now I'd like to share those lessons and tools with you. I recommend taking notes as you read each chapter—in digital form if you can—to make it easier for you to execute the action steps.

FULL DISCLOSURE

There are a few things you should know before getting started with your work-life optimization journey.

First, this book will not tell you to abandon what you love most about your career, nor will it attempt to diminish any of the amazing things you've already accomplished in it. Likewise, this book will not feed the unrealistic perfectionist illusion that you can achieve a ten out of ten in *every* aspect of life.

You cannot be a *perfect* leader, spouse, parent, friend, and community member. I do not advocate for perfection in all areas of life. It is an impossible venture and attempting it is a recipe for burnout. Rather, I want to help you become an eight or nine out of ten in the areas—professional and personal—that matter *most* to you.

Second, I would be seriously remiss if I did not mention that I stand on the shoulders of giants who have published numerous outstanding works about many of the key concepts and lessons in these chapters. I have built my approach by adapting some of the most profound thoughts and actions of the remarkable people who wrote them.

Adding my perspective, experience, and applications to these ideas has led to inspiring results for CEOs and other leaders. You will read about some of the positive outcomes in the chapters that follow. My hope is that sharing the knowledge that helped those people will allow you and countless others to see a clearer path to work-life optimization.

It's also important to understand that I am not a medical or mental health professional, nor do I know your individual circumstances. Everyone is different, but I understand what it's like to have your personal and professional lives out of balance.

Finally, whereas the core message of every story in this book is 100 percent true, some names, dates, places, and other minor details have been altered to protect the anonymity and/or confidentiality of the people mentioned. Rest assured that *nothing* in these pages is scandalous in even the slightest way. Rather, the vignettes in each chapter are meant to inspire and motivate.

Your first steps toward true self-actualization begin with fully buying in, figuring out exactly what you want, and knowing where you currently stand with the things you want most in life. Let's dive in!

CHAPTER 1

WHAT MATTERS?

"In fact, if I'm happy at work, I'm better at home—a better husband and better father. And if I'm happy at home, I come into work more energized—a better employee and a better colleague."

—Jeff Bezos, founder, executive chairman, and former CEO of Amazon

True self-actualization stems from becoming an eight or nine out of ten in the several facets of life that matter most to you.

Venture capital (VC) firms often refer me to coach a founder or CEO of one of their portfolio companies. The first step in our process is to see if my coaching style aligns with the CEO's goals.

I explain my philosophy of helping leaders to get the most out of their careers, grow their businesses, *and* enjoy a high quality of life. When I get to that last part, sometimes it becomes abundantly clear that the person truly wants to live in their office, develop the most dominant company in the world, and be considered the greatest CEO of all time. They have no problem blowing up every other area of their life to get to where they want to be professionally. (At least, they *think* they won't have a problem with it.)

Those engagements are easy for me to turn down. Fortunately, this is not representative of the typical business leader. Most CEOs and others in high-profile positions want more. They want phenomenal business growth, but also to enhance the personal lives of themselves, their loved ones, and their teammates.

- They want to scale their business by creating a culture that attracts, retains, and develops "A" players while making improvements for future generations.
- They want to create long-lasting respect and appreciation for their brand by positively impacting local communities and charitable organizations.
- They also want to achieve presence, deepen connections, and strengthen relationships with family, friends, and others.
- They want to achieve solid mental and physical health.
- Ultimately, they want to have a manageable degree of balance in their lives.

Easier said than done? You bet. For several reasons, many leaders find it difficult to achieve a robust, multifaceted lifestyle.

For starters, their leadership habits may have been shaped by an autocratic boss or controlling role model. Old habits die hard, especially when few team members are willing to risk upsetting them with criticism. A few other common issues:

- They aren't attracting and retaining enough top-notch talent, who have more choices for employment in a more remote and hybrid-friendly economy. The culture often doesn't meet the needs of the younger generation's distinctly different priorities. They may have employees who are valuable contributors but are harmful to the culture. This could drive away much-needed additional talent.
- They spend time in suboptimal ways. Some leaders hesitate to delegate less important tasks and spend too much time deep

in the weeds and putting out lower-level fires. This makes it difficult, if not impossible, to dedicate enough time to deep strategic thinking about topics like innovation, markets, and mergers and acquisitions (M&A).

- They feel tremendous pressure and isolation without many trusted allies. Opening up to colleagues or board members poses a risk, while therapists and life partners lack the business experience to truly understand their problems.

Perhaps the most difficult challenge for some of the leaders I work with is overcoming their perfectionism. They're trying to achieve a ten out of ten in every area of life, which is impossible. So, they feel compelled to cut back on professional or personal areas. Guilt prevents them from prioritizing their personal lives for two reasons. First, they're concerned that their team may think they're not working as hard as everyone else. Second, they worry about losing their ability to maximize performance versus their competition. As a result, the personal areas of life suffer. High stress, poor sleep habits, and not enough time for exercise have undesirable outcomes. Frustration and impatience quickly lead to outbursts with the people they care about most. The demand to always be at the top of their professional game causes a lack of presence with family members and strained relationships with others. Eventually, burnout ensues, making it even more difficult to achieve the balance they so desperately desire.

Countless leaders, just like you, want solutions to all these problems under one condition: nothing can impede their progress toward achieving lofty career goals. This book provides answers to those problems that don't require giving up ambitious professional aspirations.

Perhaps you're open to learning more about the benefits of leading without burnout but you need some data and personal anecdotes to solidify your buy-in. Let's start with the true story of someone who affected millions of people with her writing about the regrets of the dying.

REGRET ME NOT

Bronnie Ware was a palliative care nurse for seven years. She wrote a viral blog post about the top deathbed regrets she heard, which turned into the bestselling book *The Top Five Regrets of the Dying.*

There are three regrets from her original post that I would like to highlight.

1. *"I wish I hadn't worked so hard."* She notes that all of the men she nursed deeply regretted spending so much of their lives on the treadmill of a work existence, missing their children's youth and their partner's companionship.
2. *"I wish I had stayed in touch with my friends."* Ware says many had deep regrets about not giving friendships the time and effort they deserved, having become so caught up in their own lives that they let golden friendships slip by over the years.
3. *"I wish that I had let myself be happier."* Many stayed stuck in old patterns and habits, as fear of change had them pretending to others, and themselves, that they were content. Many didn't realize until the end that happiness is a choice.

Ware isn't the only one to provide proof that, in the end, most of us wish we had focused more of our time on personal matters, not financial or professional ones. United HealthCare polled centenarians and found that compared to those who regretted not making more money, nearly twice as many wished they had focused more on relationships and had taken better care of themselves.

These takeaways are especially relevant since we're in the midst of a tremendous mental health crisis impacting not just employees but business leaders as well. A recent survey by Deloitte showed that

70 percent of C-suite executives are seriously considering quitting for a job that better supports their well-being.[1] The model of *working harder than anyone else* clearly isn't as beneficial as we might think it is.

I've made similar discoveries with my own clients and friends. Recently, I was speaking with the founder of a multibillion-dollar real estate fund that posted incredible returns and generated significant wealth for their family. The problem was the cost of working a hundred hours a week. Consequently, they missed their children's most cherished events and were stressed and distracted even when they were physically present. The constant influx of emails and phone calls made it impossible for them to be mentally available for others.

One night, this person and their spouse had some friends over who were in a radically different financial situation. Over the course of a dinner conversation, they were struck by how much happier their friends were despite struggling to pay their bills.

This was a life-changing wake-up call. Fortunately, they realized that changes were needed long before Ware's palliative care patients did.

They chose a different path—one that led to more happiness. They decided to shut down their fund and set up a new type of investment structure through a family office. This allowed them to spend more quality time with their family, slash their stress, and experience intellectual growth from exploring asset classes beyond real estate.

One of the biggest discoveries they made was that this level of wealth did not have the massive impact on happiness they thought it did. They aren't the only ones. In fact, research from highly reputable sources proves it.

> *"We all have at least the potential to make more money in the future, we can never go back and recapture time that is now gone. So it makes no sense to let opportunities pass us by for fear of squandering our money. Squandering our lives should be a much greater worry."*
>
> —Bill Perkins, author of *Die with Zero*

HOW MUCH DOES MONEY DRIVE HAPPINESS?

In *Don't Trust Your Gut*, former Google data scientist Seth Stephens-Davidowitz uses hard data to show where conventional wisdom is wrong in many areas of life. With regard to happiness, he looks at several different studies.

For starters, Matthew Killingsworth of the University of Pennsylvania conducted a study that challenged the popular theory that there is zero effect on happiness above an income of $75,000 per year.[2] Further examination of his work concluded the following:

1. People who equated money with success were less happy than those who didn't.
2. High earners reported feeling far more stressed about time.
3. Only people who already consider themselves happy achieve incremental increases in happiness as their income increases above $75,000.

Laurie Santos, the famous professor of a "happiness" course at Yale, interpreted the results of his initial study by saying, "For the amount of work you have to put in to sextuple your income, you could instead just write in a gratitude journal, or you could sleep an extra hour."

In my experience, many high earners overemphasize net worth as a reflection of their self-worth. When they see their net worth level up, they get a fleeting sugar high in an ego boost. Once the buzz wears off, they move the financial goalposts yet again. Thus the cycle of endlessly chasing unattainable fulfillment from earning more and more money continues.

Santos also provided robust insight into our relationship with time and money in an interview from 2019.[3] During the talk, she highlighted work from Ashley Whillians, a professor at Harvard Business School. Her study found that most of us are inclined to give up time to get more money, but the opposite is actually true: When we give up money to get time, we become happier.

One of the world's foremost experts on longevity, Dr. Peter Attia, made a similar observation regarding the tradeoff of health for wealth. In his book, *Outlive*, Attia states that once many of his patients (who are often longtime executives) reach a certain age, they often realize that they have it all wrong. After many years of neglecting well-being to focus on financial status, they start to feel constant pain and other consequences from being in bad shape, signaling a not-so-bright future of frequent and severe health problems. For many, this is a breaking point. Do they continue on their current path, or do they try to prioritize health before it's too late?

Happiness now and in retirement years is at stake. Are you realistically on track to fulfill those dreams of global travel, community involvement, time spent with family, or whatever your vision is? Or are you on a path to spend extensive time at the doctor's office, in the hospital, or worse?

Another study of thousands of millionaires led by researchers at Harvard Business School did find a gain in happiness that kicks in when people's net worth rises above $8 million. But the effect was small: A net worth of $8 million offers a boost of happiness that is roughly half as large as the happiness boost from being married.

The Mappiness Project, founded by British economists Susana Mourato and George MacKerron, collected three million data points to "map" happiness over space and time. It found the activities that make people happiest include sex, exercise, and gardening. People get a big happiness boost from being with a romantic partner or friends. People are consistently happier when they are out in nature, particularly near a body of water, or when the scenery is beautiful.

Davidovitz's conclusion: "The data-driven answer to life is as follows: Be with your love, on an eighty-degree and sunny day, overlooking a beautiful body of water, while having sex."

FIND OUT WHAT YOU WANT MOST

"You can't have everything you want, but you can have the things that really matter to you."

—Marissa Mayer, former CEO of Yahoo
and Google's first female engineer

We were not put on this planet, nor is it worth it, to maximize every dollar and become the Greatest of All Time (GOAT) at our professional craft if it comes at the expense (and it does) of every other aspect of life. It is impossible to be the best leader, spouse, parent, friend, and philanthropist while maintaining excellent physical and mental health. You can't be everything to everyone, but you can be great at the things that matter most to you.

To fully understand how important balance is (or is not) to you, start with something I call the Bar Conversation test.

If two friends are talking at a bar and your name comes up, what do you hope to hear about yourself?

The first option is that one of them says, "Oh yeah, they are extremely sharp. They've done well in their career, have a close relationship with their kids, and have a solid marriage. Last I heard, they were on several nonprofit boards where they care deeply about the causes. I think they still play golf on the weekends with their friends too. It seems like they have a *lot* going for them."

Or would you rather hear:

"I can't believe what they've accomplished in their career. They have made an obscene amount of money! Too bad I heard their personal life fell apart. Their kids barely talk to them anymore. They ended up having a number of health issues you usually don't see until much later in life. I get how it happened, though. They can't even have a conversation that doesn't revolve around work or making more money."

If you've read this far, you most likely prefer the first option. If for some reason, the second sounds more appealing, this book may not be for you.

Now that we've squared that away, let's figure out what matters most to you. Everyone is different. Even other high-performing leaders have divergent areas of their life they want to optimize. To figure out what you really want, answer the following questions from a vision and values exercise I give to my coaching clients as a foundation for our work.

- What is your long-term vision of professional success? Think bigger than just you. What would long-term success for your business life look like? For example, what goals would you and your team hit?
- Dig deep into why you chose that vision of professional success and business growth. What specific core values of yours influenced your answers?
- What would it feel like to achieve that vision? What would it feel like to fail at it?

- What is your long-term vision of personal success? Think bigger than just you. What would long-term success for your relationships and family life look like? For example, what personal goals would you or those closest to you achieve?
- Dig deep into why you chose that vision for personal and family success. What specific core values of yours influenced your answers?
- What would it feel like to achieve that vision? What would it feel like to fail at it?
- Picture your future self in a retirement setting. You have a lot of time to sit outside and reflect on life. Looking back on your dream life with no major regrets, what does it look like?

The next step is to see where you stand on those desired goals by referencing the Wheel of Life image and completing the associated exercise I'm about to describe.

The Wheel of Life was originally created by Paul J. Meyer, the founder of the Success Motivation Institute. I have adapted it to reflect the demands and wants of today's business leaders.

WHEEL OF LIFE

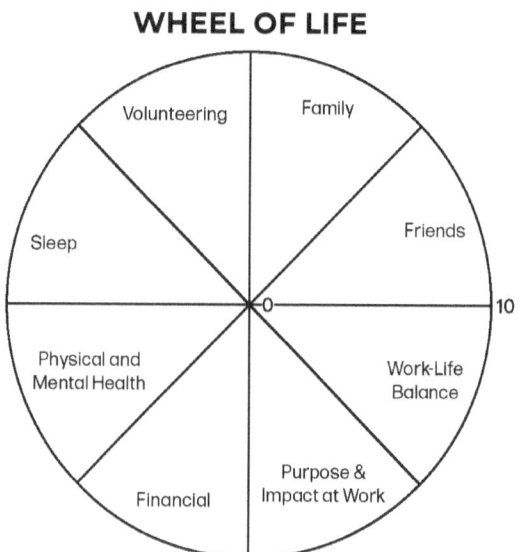

By looking at the associated image, you see eight areas of life—Family, Friends, Work-Life Balance, Purpose and Impact at Work, Financial, Physical and Mental Health, Sleep, and Volunteering—that can contribute to enhanced overall well-being.

Rate how well you're doing in each area of life. Draw a line from the center, which represents zero, to the edge, which represents ten. Stop where you think your rating would be. For example, if you think you rate a five in work-life balance, you would draw a line from the center halfway to the edge of the wheel. When you're done with each line of the wheel, ask yourself some questions.

- How balanced is your wheel?
- In what categories are you rating lower than you would like?
- How much does each of these categories matter to you?
- For each category you already rate highly or want to rate higher, why did you rate them the way you did?

Now compare your conclusions from the vision and values exercise to where you rate in the Wheel of Life. Where are the disconnects? Why?

> *"I believe a balanced life is essential, and I try to make sure that all of our employees know that and live that way."*
>
> **—Marc Benioff, CEO of Salesforce**

Remember, everybody ranks the importance of these eight categories differently. For example, you might rate yourself a three on volunteering, but that might not be a priority for you at this stage of your life. The goal is to be an eight or nine out of ten in the categories that matter most to you now or over the next twelve months.

From a personal perspective, my wheel is the most balanced it's ever been due to some of the tools in this book. This is also the happiest and most fulfilled I've ever been. By doing this exercise, I've realized that the family and friends categories matter most to me. So, I drop my kids off at school every day and make sure to hug them tight. I also have weekly lunches with my mom and stepdad and often host barbecues and sports viewing events for friends and family.

Just because those things make me happy and fulfilled doesn't mean they will be what matters most to you. They might still be valuable, but only rate a six. Maybe health rates a nine for you and you need to focus on that most. Everyone's wheel is different.

The final step in the Wheel of Life exercise is the most important, but you should finish the book first to maximize its effectiveness. For now, put a note on your calendar for a few weeks ahead. Write the specific actions you will commit to for the next twelve months to improve on the categories that matter most to you. Put the action steps on your daily to-do list, calendar, or anywhere else that will remind you to execute on them. I ask my clients to complete the Wheel of Life exercise annually to stay accountable to their evolving goals.

> "By all means, pursue your success. Realize your ambition. Just make sure it's not coming at the cost of what actually matters. Looking at Marcus (Aurelius), however, we can see that you don't have to choose. You can run one of the biggest empires in history and still come home to kiss your children."
>
> —Ryan Holiday, author of *The Daily Stoic*

CALM YOUR GUILT

At this point, you might be starting to embrace the idea of leading without burnout, but lingering feelings of guilt might be preventing total buy-in. You might fear that your teams will resent or disrespect you for not working hard enough. You might also feel guilty about possibly losing your professional edge and ability to outperform the competition.

If you create the culture I outline in this book, your people will fully support your personal growth and take great pride in executing as well as possible for you.

It might seem counterintuitive, but focusing on nonprofessional areas that matter to you will actually increase the odds of successfully scaling your business. Imagine what it will feel like to achieve true self-actualization as you become an eight or nine out of ten in the facets of life that matter most to you without diminishing your professional success.

You've now gained an understanding of the potential in developing personal vision and values. In the next chapter, you'll see how to create that for your organization with detailed cultural bylaws, which are far more impactful than traditional values and mission statements.

"We think, mistakenly, that success is the result of the amount of time we put in at work, instead of the quality of time we put in."

—Arianna Huffington, CEO of Thrive Global

LEAD WITHOUT BURNOUT

▶ Most leaders want to balance professional growth and business scalability with a happy family life and good physical and mental health.

▶ An array of data and personal anecdotes show that regret is more often related to relationships and quality of life, rather than professional accolades or financial status.

▶ Use the vision and values exercise to help you figure out what you want most out of life.

▶ Use the Wheel of Life exercise to see where you currently stand on your key priorities and determine how you can execute better on them.

CHAPTER 2

CULTURAL BYLAWS

"People don't buy what you do; they buy why you do it. And what you do simply proves what you believe."

—Simon Sinek, author and inspirational speaker

Your team members may not be buying into the company's mission statement, vision, and core values the way you want them to.

A staggering 61 percent of employees don't know their company's mission statement. Among those who are familiar with it, 57 percent say it doesn't motivate them.[4] Additional research shows that nearly half of American employees don't know the values of the company for which they work.[5]

From what I've learned in my work with CEOs in both a group setting and one-on-one, most leaders want to scale their business beyond themselves. Yet, they feel growing pains because they get stuck deep in the weeds of too many decisions. They know they must trust others to execute on the details but find it difficult. To do this successfully, you need to establish a culture that attracts and retains "A" players throughout the organization. In today's world, that might be harder than ever before.

Top talent has choices they never had before, because some employers are now embracing more remote or hybrid work situations. Additionally, however you built cultures in the past may not work with younger generations who have different priorities around mental health, flexibility, and work-life optimization.

Even if you are able to land and keep "A" players across your staff, you must address the new realities involved in a hybrid/remote workforce. Those talented team members often work different hours from all over the world. Years ago, productive communication was as simple as walking down the hallway and into someone's office. Now, you might need to send a direct message, wait for a reply, and book a time for a video conference.

Traditional mission statements, core values, and visions don't address these nuances of the modern workforce. They might look motivational on the surface, but unless you build a culture that "walks the talk," they're just words.

We already mentioned some eye-opening inefficiencies concerning the percentages of employees who don't know the mission statement, aren't motivated by it, and can't recall their company's values. Let's dive deeper into the numbers…

According to a recent Gallup poll, only one in every four employees believes in their company's values.[6]

In a separate study conducted by MIT's Sloan School of Management, no correlation was found between the company values emphasized in published statements and how well the company lived up to those values in the eyes of its employees.[7]

Perhaps most importantly, 63 percent of employees don't have a clear understanding of what their company is trying to do and why.[8]

THE REASONS MISSION STATEMENTS HAVE LARGELY FAILED

"Our challenge is to assertively network economically sound methods of empowerment so that we may continually negotiate performance-based infrastructures."

—Dilbert mission statement generator

The biggest problem with traditional mission statements is that they don't communicate anything tangible. They usually contain fuzzy buzzwords, trendy industry jargon, and vague (often generic) language. Most of them lack differentiation.

American Standard's former mission statement was to "Be the best in the eyes of our customers, employees, and shareholders."

While "being the best" is certainly a noble and worthwhile endeavor, what does it even mean? In what ways, within those relationships, do you want to be the best, and how are you going to do it?

Hershey's previous mission statement was to have "undisputed marketplace leadership."

Both of those mission statements are subjective, lack specific action steps, and fail to give employees clarity on what matters the most.

Additionally, mission statements are often formed by top-tier executives without input from those in the trenches. These mission statements often don't reflect reality or inspire shared meaning. How are team members going to rally behind your

If you're a CEO, it's also great for you to encourage teams to have their own bylaws as long as they don't conflict with the larger vision of the company. If you're not a CEO, get the OK from your boss to execute cultural bylaws for your team and apply what you learn in this chapter.

cause and work collaboratively if you're not including their input in shaping your mission statement?

Is your mission statement specific, where team members understand what matters most and how exactly to proceed?

What percentage of your team members had input in shaping the mission statement?

With the proven inefficiencies of traditional mission statements and the core values that support them, consider using something different and much more comprehensive. By establishing cultural bylaws instead, you will give employees more clear and concrete priorities, and better tools for taking action and making sound decisions. You will also inspire shared meaning and be better equipped to appeal to the younger generation's "A" players. They will more readily identify your business as a place they want to grow, support, and embody the values. To establish effective cultural bylaws, you must develop four critical sections. Start by answering three questions: Why, what, and how?

WHY?

> *"We are drawn to leaders and organizations that are good at communicating what they believe. Their ability to make us feel like we belong, to make us feel special, safe, and not alone, is part of what gives them the ability to inspire us."*
>
> —Simon Sinek, author and motivational speaker

Most of Sinek's wildly popular book, *Start with Why*, focuses on marketing and attracting customers, but a small part of it is profoundly insightful for landing top talent—the why as it relates to hiring.

A big part of human nature is the desire to belong to something bigger than ourselves—something that symbolizes our values and beliefs. You see this all the time in politics, religion, consumerism, and most recently, the company people work for. A recent survey from LinkedIn found the vast majority of Gen Z professionals, 87 percent, would be prepared to quit their jobs to work elsewhere if the values of the new company were more closely aligned with theirs.[9]

Just as differentiation is crucial when marketing to customers, you need to stand out when recruiting top talent. This is especially important given that other firms may be able to offer equal to greater compensation and/or brand name prestige. Consider referencing the "why" portion of your cultural bylaws on job descriptions as a differentiator in attracting the right people for you.

World-renowned behavioral psychologist Robert Cialdini lists seven principles of persuasion. One of them, the "liking" principle, states that people are more likely to like you if you like them. You can use this to your advantage in the interview process. Tell the best candidates you really like them because they fit so well with your cultural bylaws and they will be more apt to like you. Hand them a copy of those bylaws so they can be reminded of your common ground when mulling over your offer. Top talent who align with your cultural bylaws become intrinsically motivated to join your cause and exceed expectations in their roles.

You could list anywhere from three to ten "whys" in your cultural bylaws. Six examples to get you started on outlining your company's purpose are as follows.

Contribute to solid financial situations for our families, charities, and investors.

A less carefully constructed core value might provide a generic one-word answer like *prosperity*. The skeptic or the cynic will assume the value is only referring to wealth for leadership and investors if you don't specifically mention others.

Maximize intellectual growth and avoid complacency.

You've gotten to where you are today by continuously learning and growing. A cultural bylaw that emphasizes these elements of success will naturally attract "A" players because most of them have similarly endless thirsts for knowledge.

Feel connection, purpose, and meaning in growing something together that is bigger than any individual.

Collaborating for impactful results is a top motivator for talent in a company culture.

Attract, win, and develop talent to enable maximum career potential, which also improves the business for future generations and provides a positive legacy.

Whether you're a CEO, VP, or another executive, you want to leave the business in a better position than when you started. Your professional legacy is at stake. Getting "A" players in the door, developing them, and maximizing their career potential is a big part of that. Even if team members grow and leave your company, that still adds to your legacy and the company's reputation through word of mouth.

Have a positive impact on communities by donating to charities and consistently creating jobs with purpose, growth, and competitive compensation.

The more profits your company makes, the more jobs you can create and the more money you can redistribute to worthy causes. If you can donate to charities that also embody some of the other cultural bylaws you establish, even better.

We will always encourage and support the mental and physical health, internal and external relationships, and work-life optimization of all team members.

You want everyone in your organization to work hard, but you also want to let them know that they cannot be fulfilled or perform at their best if other areas of their life are suffering. Let existing and prospective team members know you have their back by not just mentioning, but by really living this crucial cultural bylaw.

Selling your company to top-tier talent means connecting with them emotionally. Develop a great story behind these answers to your "why." Then, tell your story to candidates during interviews and see with whom it resonates.

A good example of storytelling to win people over is how charities and universities seeking donations often highlight the story of one person who has benefited from past charitable gifts. The purpose is to form an emotional connection that influences the decision-making of possible donors. You can do the same with your potential team members.

"The most powerful person in the world is the storyteller."

—Steve Jobs, cofounder, former
CEO, and chairman of Apple Inc.

WHAT?

You've seen several examples of answering your "why" in your cultural bylaws to attract "A" players. Next up is what you do. This is where you articulate your strategic vision of what you're trying to do to solve your key constituents' problems. When addressing the "what," you're speaking about team members, customers, investors, suppliers, vendors, and others depending on the nature of your business.

The goal is to find "whats" that meet the desires of your constituents with your own broader goals. It's a fine balance. You want to be specific with revenue targets, the desired size of the team, geographies, new markets to enter, and/or other OKRs while not giving away anything confidential.

You could list anywhere from three to ten "whats" in your cultural bylaws. For example, a chief investment officer or portfolio manager of a hedge fund whose "customers" are investors might design something like this.

Deliver superior risk-adjusted returns, exceeding 15 percent annually.

Investors are always trying to find consistent investment vehicles with strong returns.

Grow to $2 billion in Assets Under Management (AUM) over the next five years.

Team members want to know they're part of a company that is growing, and they want to know what to expect for that growth over a specific period of time.

Increase to five the number of subsectors we know well enough to invest in: U.S. retail, international retail, restaurants, consumer packaged goods (CPG), and e-commerce.

Investors are looking for investment firms that are aware of the need to diversify risk and grow opportunities.

Expand the investment team to five analysts, each of whom will provide support in one of the five subsectors.

Growing and mentoring talent is a personally fulfilling aspect of a leader's role. Also, a goal related to job creation and talent development is usually cast in a favorable light with all constituents.

Donate X percent of profits to XYZ charitable organizations.

You said that giving back to charities was a key motivator in the "why" of your cultural bylaws. Here you can be more specific about what you're going to do by calling out charities that are aligned with your brand.

Establish a world-class culture in fostering mental health and work-life optimization.

Most of the top talent, particularly those of the younger generations, are looking to work for companies that support the emotional well-being of everyone.

Notice how each of the sample cultural bylaws related to "what" addresses a particular constituent, such as investors and team members.

HOW?

After you answer the "why" and the "what" of your company, you can tell everyone *how* you plan to achieve your vision. Map out the core strengths and identity of your team. Tell people about the philosophies that will get the team to where it wants to be. The 1985 Chicago Bears and 2000 Baltimore Ravens hung their hats on defense and toughness. What is your team's identity?

Warren Buffett has become one of the wealthiest people in the world by investing in businesses that have durable competitive advantages, strong management teams, and are trading at a discount to intrinsic value. If you look back at your company history, in what specific situations have you thrived?

You could list anywhere from three to ten "hows" in your cultural bylaws. Continuing with the hedge fund example, this is what some of their "hows" might look like.

Know our companies better than all other investors by committing to the highest standards for depth and quality of research.

This answers anybody's question about how the company will generate returns.

Find a new angle that will change a company's profits to be at least 10 percent higher than consensus expectations. The stock should have less than 15 percent downside or a return potential that is at least three times higher than the downside risk.

This gives more specifics about the type of investments analysts should be seeking and investors should be expecting.

Trust and empower our teammates with the autonomy to own higher-level tasks or projects.

This should be a part of every leader's "how." There is no other way to achieve work-life balance and grow your business. It is one of the most important lessons in this book and the focus of Chapter 3.

Solve hard problems together with open debate, where we assume everyone has positive intentions. Everyone will feel heard, respected, and be given high-candor feedback.

This is also a crucial "how" for any leader and the subject of Chapter 4. Collaboration with good intentions and honest, productive feedback is an extension of trusting your "A" players to do great work.

Bolster the mental health of all team members with regular check-ins, empathetic listening, recognition of efforts, and decisions that facilitate work-life optimization.

These are specific action steps about how you will prioritize the mental health of your team members. It's not enough to just say you value something; you need to take actionable steps to prove it. Chapter 5 will provide more detail.

Commit to executing each of our world-class due diligence practices to recruit, hire, and develop "A" players who fit our culture.

Chapter 6 details how to land "A" players. Mentioning it in your "who," "what," and "how" shows the importance of this cultural bylaw.

Do the honest, right, and fair thing, even if it means a less favorable outcome.

Just about every company lists integrity as a value, but almost nobody can tell you what it actually means in practice. This cultural bylaw explains how you will display integrity in simple language. And yes, these hedge funds do exist! I was blessed to work for two of them.

LESSONS LEARNED

Perhaps more important than your successes are the lessons learned from previous mistakes. Incorporate these into your cultural bylaws to avoid repeating them. Here are a few lessons I learned from mistakes I made when I was a hedge fund investor that are applicable to other business decisions.

Sometimes our conviction score for a potential investment, acquisition, or other initiative ranks below an eight out of ten. Those situations have usually been a wash at best and a huge negative weight on returns, time, and mental energy at worst.

Before you started researching this situation, did you already have a thesis or desire to go in one direction? As you researched it, did you downplay information that went against your original thesis? Did you seek out or cherry-pick information that would support your original thesis? Instead, you must dispassionately gather and evaluate evidence on both sides of the situation.

Are you relying too heavily on recent short-term trends? Are you extrapolating recent profitability despite the cyclicality of the industry or business cycles? Are you assuming current valuations will always be the norm? Ensure you're getting a strong ROI across full, longer-term cycles.

Have you been sticking with a struggling division, employee, or other investment that you know in your heart was a mistake? Is this situation unlikely to turn around? Focus more on limiting future losses and less on trying to recoup sunk costs. Would divesting or moving on relieve a big ongoing weight on your capital, time, or mental energy?

When evaluating a past decision, focus on the process behind it, not the outcome from it. Outcomes can be highly influenced by luck, randomness, and other factors out of your control. Perhaps the research and decision process was sound, and the downside case happened to play out. If there was a mistake in the process, how do you fix it? What lesson can you add to this checklist so you don't repeat it?

After you've completed the four sections of your cultural bylaws, you should have a document that looks something like this:

XYZ CAPITAL MANAGEMENT BYLAWS

WHY (purpose)

- Contribute to solid financial situations for our families, charities, and investors.
- Maximize intellectual growth and avoid complacency.
- Feel connection, purpose, and meaning in growing something together that is bigger than any individual.
- Attract, win, and develop talent to enable maximum career potential, which also improves the business for future generations and provides a positive legacy.
- Have a positive impact on communities by donating to charities and consistently creating jobs with purpose, growth, and competitive salary.
- We will always encourage and support the mental and physical health, internal and external relationships, and work-life optimization of all team members.

WHAT (strategic vision)

- Deliver superior risk-adjusted returns, exceeding 15 percent annually.
- Grow to $2 billion in Assets Under Management (AUM) over the next five years.

- Increase to five the number of subsectors we know well enough to invest in: U.S. retail, international retail, restaurants, consumer packaged goods (CPG), and e-commerce.
- Expand the investment team to five analysts, each of whom will provide support in one of the five subsectors.
- Donate X percent of profits to XYZ charitable organizations.
- Establish a world-class culture in fostering mental health and work-life optimization.

HOW (identity for success)

- Know our companies better than all other investors by committing to the highest standards for depth and quality of research.
- Find a new angle that will change a company's profits to be at least 10 percent higher than consensus expects. The stock should have less than 15 percent downside, or a return potential that is at least three times higher than the downside risk.
- Trust and empower our teammates with the autonomy to own higher-level tasks or projects.
- Solve hard problems together with open debate, where we assume everyone has positive intentions. Everyone will feel heard, respected, and be given high-candor feedback.
- Bolster the mental health of all team members with regular check-ins, empathetic listening, recognition of efforts, and decisions that facilitate work-life optimization.
- Commit to executing each of our world-class due diligence practices to recruit, hire, and develop "A" players who fit our culture.
- Do the honest, right, and fair thing, even if it means a less favorable outcome.

LESSONS LEARNED

- Sometimes our conviction score for a potential investment, acquisition, or other initiative ranks below an eight out of ten. Those situations have usually been a wash at best and a huge negative weight on returns, time, and mental energy at worst.

- Before you started researching this situation, did you already have a thesis or desire to go in one direction? As you researched it, did you downplay information that went against your original thesis? Did you seek out or cherry-pick information that would support your original thesis? Instead, you must dispassionately gather and evaluate evidence on both sides of the situation.

- Are you relying too heavily on recent short-term trends? Are you extrapolating recent profitability despite the cyclicality of the industry or business cycles? Are you assuming current valuations will always be the norm? Ensure you are getting a strong ROI across full, longer-term cycles.

- Have you been sticking with a struggling division, employee, or other investment that you know in your heart was a mistake? Is this situation unlikely to turn around? Focus more on limiting future losses and less on trying to recoup sunk costs. Would divesting or moving on relieve a big ongoing weight on your capital, time, or mental energy?

- When evaluating a past decision, focus on the process behind it, not the outcome from it. Outcomes can be highly influenced by luck, randomness, and other factors out of your control. Perhaps the research and decision process was sound, and the downside case happened to play out. If there was a mistake in the process, how do you fix it? What lesson can you add to this checklist so you don't repeat it?

Dated: _____

_____
RYAN RENTERIA, PORTFOLIO MANAGER

RANK YOUR PRIORITIES AND CONSTITUENTS

In a hybrid workplace where you're trying to scale the business and get tasks off your plate and onto the "A" players you trust, you may consider ranking your constituents—customers, team members, suppliers, community, investors—within your bylaws. Granted, all of them are important, but establishing an order of prioritization helps your team make decisions without you. You can do this implicitly with how you order each bylaw or explicitly in its own bylaw.

A good example of ranking constituents comes from the Costco cult loved by so many shoppers. Due to the products and value proposition they offer, they have not only gained appreciation from their customers, but also from their own team members. A big part of that love fest comes from their leadership.

During my time on Wall Street, I got to know the leadership team of Costco, led by CEO Jim Sinegal. Forbes ranked Jim as one of America's favorite leaders with a 93-percent employee approval rating.

Jim had a specific ranking system of priorities that started with "obey the law." In terms of constituents, customers were always first in his vision. He did this at the risk of being seen unfavorably by Wall St. analysts. We doubted some of his policies. For example, Jim supported a cap on the gross profit margin Costco could earn on their products. If the company was able to save a lot of money by negotiating better terms with suppliers, they typically passed the savings on to the customer through lower pricing, rather than letting it fall to the company's bottom line.

The company also had a liberal return policy. Unfortunately, this act of goodwill was abused by a small percentage of people. Nonetheless, the customers loved it. They also appreciated the continual improvement in value from Costco's pricing philosophy. The result was a ridiculously high membership renewal rate year after year. That predictable income stream helped drive significant growth in their net profits, as loyal customers purchased more and spread the word.

Number two on Jim's ranking of constituents were the team members. Jim always paid the team members much higher wages than the industry average. He also provided them with world-class healthcare and other benefits. On the surface, this might seem like a lot of money that could have been re-invested elsewhere. Once again, Jim had Costco's priorities right. The net result was one of the lowest turnover rates and theft rates in the industry.

By ranking customers and team members at the top of his constituent priority list, Jim created raving fans across the country. Costco didn't just have shoppers, they had die-hards who would renew their membership every year. The company didn't simply have team members; it had loyalists who took pride and excelled in everything they did, which contributed even further to the great customer experience.

> *"Imagine having 120,000 loyal ambassadors out there, constantly saying good things about the company. It has to be a significant advantage."*
>
> **– Jim Sinegal, cofounder and former CEO of Costco**

The company's suppliers received a beneficial increase in their product sales in conjunction with Costco's growth.

Communities were also thrilled to be a part of the Costco fan base, as they reaped the rewards of quality local jobs.

Investors? Well, they actually weren't on the ranked list of constituents at all. Nonetheless, the company outperformed the competition and crushed the S&P 500 over a long period of time. One of the greatest mistakes of my investing career was not owning Costco's stock in greater size and for a longer period of time.

By clearly ranking Costco's priorities and constituents, Jim Sinegal took the pressures from Wall St. off of his C-suite and helped them make sound decisions.

GETTING EVERYONE TO BUY INTO YOUR CULTURAL BYLAWS

There are several ways to get everyone to buy into your cultural bylaws. I have outlined some of the most effective below.

TEAM MEMBER SURVEYS

A key element of getting buy-in for bylaws and establishing a deeper tie to your culture is by surveying team members about them. When team members are asked to help shape bylaws through surveys, they feel heard and valued. This will also help them to understand how they're contributing to something bigger than themselves.

By surveying team members, you're following the Cialdini Unity principle, part of which is that people like people more when they create something together.

The following seven questions could be used as examples of what your survey could look like.

- What do you think our purpose is?
- What motivates you to work here?
- What are the biggest problems and greatest desires of our customers? What are your top ideas to address those issues?
- What big opportunities do you think we should be focused on, and what specifically would you like to see us achieve long-term?
- What are the core strengths that will help us get there?
- Where are we falling short that could prevent us from achieving those areas of focus, and what could we do to improve?
- What mistakes have we made and how can we avoid them in the future?

After you've compiled the surveys, explain to everyone how you incorporated their feedback into the bylaws and made appropriate changes.

As critical as it is to know the positive results of making team members feel heard, it is equally important to understand how disappointed and demotivated they get when they take the time to provide feedback, don't see it reflected, and feel unheard.

SHOW, DON'T TELL

Making people feel heard is important, but a prerequisite to buy-in of cultural bylaws is to show people how they work by living them.

You and other leaders must emulate the cultural bylaws. Think of it like a parent wanting your child to exhibit patience, kindness, and respect for others. If you model those qualities in your life, the chances are much greater that your child will reflect what they see. My CEO coaching business has a reciprocal benefit, as I often learn as much from my clients as they do from me. One of them, who is a phenomenal father of three adult children, once astutely told me, "Your kids listen to 10 percent of what you say, but they observe 100 percent of what you do."

Read the bylaws and identify the top three changes you, personally, can make to better live by them. Tell team members about the action steps you will take, and ask everyone to hold you accountable with candid feedback.

Soliciting feedback should be a two-part process. First, it should be given in the moment. If someone catches you not living by the expectations you've set forth, they should feel empowered to tell you about it. When they do, make a note of it on your phone, computer, or piece of paper. Thank the team member for providing you with the observation. Second, review those cultural bylaws frequently, refer to the moments where you didn't emulate them, and write down a specific action you can take to correct that specific problem.

Another way to emulate the cultural bylaws is to show how every major action taken aligns with them. This can be just a few words. For example, if you're introducing a new mental health benefit, reference the bylaw that identifies that as an important part of who you are as a company.

You can also model the importance of cultural bylaws by hiring like-minded people. Seek out "A" players who have similar mindsets that align with the "who," "what," and "how" of your company. Develop interview questions around your bylaws to identify these people quickly in the interview process.

A CONSISTENT REFERENCE POINT

Even the best talent will need to be reminded of cultural bylaws. Let's face facts: it's easy to let routine tasks, brush fires, and long-term goals consume our workdays. Therefore, we all need visual reminders of "why," "what," and "how" we do our jobs, as well as lessons learned from previous mistakes.

Once bylaws are established, get them printed on high-quality paper, hand them out to everyone, and have everyone sign them. Nothing solicits buy-in quite like a signature. It's akin to getting someone's personal guarantee. The Cialdini Commitment principle says that people are much more likely to follow through once they've formally committed to something.

Your bylaws should serve as your identity on your office whiteboard. Ensure everyone has a digital copy that is easily accessible on their computer, and encourage everyone to keep a physical copy in their briefcase. You should be able to find them in the morning to guide your day and at various times throughout the day to refocus, especially under times of duress. It might help to think of them as an extended locker-room slogan. One of the greatest NBA coaches of all time, Greg Popovich, used the following words to describe the "how" of the San Antonio Spurs.

> *"When nothing seems to help, I go and look at a stonecutter hammering away at his rock perhaps a hundred times without as much as a crack showing in it. Yet at the hundred and first blow, it will split in two, and I know it was not that blow that did it—but all that had gone before."*
>
> —Jacob Riis, Danish-American social reformer and poet

The quote hung in the Spurs locker room to remind everyone about the importance of process. They weren't obsessing over the outcome of a win or loss. Rather, they were driven by the long-term process of how to get where they wanted to be.

Reviewing the cultural bylaws should be a regular occurrence for everyone, particularly before they form their to-do lists. When I was in the hedge fund business, the order in which I prioritized the stocks I would focus on had a massive impact on my returns. I could incur a big loss of opportunity if I chose to work on stock X first, while stock Y went up 40 percent. It helped me to have a system that prioritized what to work on first, second, etc. on any given day.

Whenever someone is writing up an idea to present, ensure they address how it fits with or violates the related cultural bylaws. When the presenter is verbally pitching the idea, this makes for great dialogue and ultimately better decision-making.

Involve team members in selecting OKRs and how their incentive compensation should be tied to them. One critical OKR should be related to how they're doing around the cultural bylaws. That can in turn become a key part of their reviews and feedback.

If you or another leader discovers a team member who embodied one of the cultural bylaws in a particularly amazing way, tell everyone about it!

"No one ever made a decision because of a number. They need a story."

—Daniel Kahneman, Israeli-American psychologist and economist

When team members hear true stories of cultural bylaws in action, they are more likely to be motivated by them and embody them. Stories have a way of bringing mere words to life.

CULTURAL BYLAWS IN ACTION

At this point, you might be thinking that the theory of replacing mission statements with cultural bylaws sounds great, but wondering if it really works. A CEO coaching client of mine provides a textbook example of how well this shift in your business's approach can work.

As part of our work on developing their cultural bylaws, my client solicited feedback from their team members. This gave my client insight from the trenches into why employees were motivated to work there, the ever-changing customer problems they must solve, and the biggest opportunities for improvement. When they emailed out the bylaws that clearly showed they incorporated employee feedback, the team members told my client they felt like valued contributors to something bigger than themselves. The bylaws also empowered team members spread out across different geographies with the tools to make more decisions without involving the CEO all the time.

My client's bylaws also emphasized maximizing team and personal growth. Those ideas resonated well with "A" players in the hiring process. When the best talent showed up for interviews where these key bylaws were discussed, they knew the culture was a great fit for their career goals. As a result, the company not only maintained the outstanding workforce they already had, but they also added exemplary people who embodied their vision and proudly put in their best efforts for a company they believed in.

Shortly after the bylaws were completed, they were honored as one of the best companies to work for in their area. Of course, that award was not received for the enactment of cultural bylaws. The CEO had already made the business a great place to work. They had already established a great culture. The bylaws just told everyone about it in a way that a traditional mission statement couldn't. What better way to model personal growth for their team members than a CEO of an already great culture investing time in cultural bylaws to make it even better?

Imagine how much better your employees will know, believe in, and embody your mission and values when they're communicated in detailed cultural bylaws that are signed and on their radar at all times. Next, you'll learn about the foundational pieces around which cultural bylaws are built.

LEAD WITHOUT BURNOUT

- ▶ Traditional mission statements and values are ineffective due to their vague, generic, and mostly undifferentiated nature.
- ▶ Develop detailed cultural bylaws with your "why," "what," and "how," and top lessons learned.
- ▶ Rank order your constituents.
- ▶ Take actionable steps to ensure team members will follow your cultural bylaws.
- ▶ Culture is more important than most leaders appreciate. Bylaws are an ideal way of teaching the culture you want to create and embedding it into everyone's actions.

CHAPTER 3

TRUST

"Trust has to be the highest value in your company, and if it's not, something bad is going to happen to you."

—Marc Benioff, CEO of Salesforce

The Conference Board reports that 70 percent of public companies experiencing a revenue stall lose more than half of their market capitalization. Additional research attributes the primary reason for these events to poor strategic decisions.[10]

Strategic thinking isn't only important for avoiding failure. It's also critical to scale your business beyond yourself. In fact, 97 percent of leaders said being strategic is the most important behavior to enable employee success.[11] Yet, 96 percent said they lacked the necessary time for strategic thinking because they were too deep in the weeds of their business.

So, strategic thinking is vital, but nobody has time for it? This is an absurd reality, but you can do something about it. The key to allotting more time for strategic thinking is the first foundational piece around which great cultural bylaws are built—trust.

To find adequate time for deep strategic thinking, you must get away from the ingrained part of your muscle memory that doesn't want to cede control. Otherwise, innovation, new markets, and the M&A necessary to scale your business will be difficult to pull off. There won't be enough time in your day to explore them properly.

THE OPPORTUNITY COST OF STAYING IN THE WEEDS

You might be thinking that being highly involved in every detail is what has driven your success throughout your career. Does it feel risky to move away from that? A ten-year study by the *Harvard Business Review* of over two thousand seven hundred newly appointed executives showed that over two-thirds of them struggled with letting go of work from previous roles.

It's possible you think that needing control over everything is just the way you are. While you might have that as a personality trait, it doesn't mean you can't evolve.

> *"Personality is not your destiny. It's your tendency. No one is limited to a single way of thinking, feeling, or acting. Who you become is not about the traits you have. It's what you decide to do with them."*
>
> **—Adam Grant, professor at Wharton, organizational psychologist, and best-selling author**

If you're resistant to changing your leadership approach because you think things are going well or it's "just the way you are," you're missing out on a massive opportunity. Balyasny has been running one of the most successful hedge funds for over twenty years. Yet, they remain laser-focused on adapting to generate even better returns.

I have seen coaches of professional sports teams win 60 percent of their games in a season. By most standards, that would be considered too successful to warrant a change of head coach. Sometimes these organizations take a risk in thinking differently, replace these successful coaches, and go on to win championships. They take a chance that they believe will make an already great team even better.

Similarly, just about every one of my CEO coaching clients has attained tremendous success, but they're doing the deep work they need to transcend their success and scale their companies to even higher levels.

Be bold in adjusting the way you think about your role and value to the company. Create a culture in which you trust your employees to do great things and they trust you to give them the freedom and resources they need to excel.

MY ENTANGLEMENT

I know what it's like to get caught in the minutiae. As my hedge fund career advanced, I doubled down on my control dysfunction.

At twenty-six years old, I was managing an expanding P&L of up to $800 million. As the assets I invested were growing, so were the stakes. I was working at an unsustainable pace and my stress level had reached a tipping point. My instinct to control everything was the opposite of what I needed to scale successfully. If I wanted to deploy a higher amount of capital, I needed to trust the analysts I had hired.

Instead, I spent way too much time checking their financial models. I often input their numbers myself because I was too afraid that they would make a mistake. If I hadn't gotten so entangled in those things, I could have spent more time thinking strategically about new market opportunities and innovations to my process. Or I could have a few extra hours to refresh my creative energy or spend time with people I cared about.

My worst performance came in the second half of 2007, when I had several months in a row of negative returns. My anxiety was running wild. This was a big wake-up call for me. My way of doing things had caused me to hit a ceiling. When I decided to loosen my grip, trust my team, and spend more time on big-picture strategy, I was able to turn things around and was fortunate to have one of my best years in 2008.

Though I recovered from these mistakes, I was disappointed that I didn't adapt faster. I wish I had used that leadership opportunity I had with those analysts to scale their careers while enhancing my personal growth much sooner. I needed to move more quickly from that obsession with every aspect of individual stocks to a more trusting leadership style. Michael Karsch was great at that. He would hire "A" players with strong expertise in their sectors and let them and their teams do detailed work. He wasn't content to simply watch them work though. He would also sit down with them, listen to their views on various investment opportunities, and use his experience to provide helpful insights and decide which should be the biggest positions in the portfolio. Karsch was a master of the big picture.

CREATING AN OPTIMIZED CULTURE

"Trust is the highest form of human motivation. It brings out the very best in people."

—Stephen Covey, American educator, author, and keynote speaker

It's hard to recognize and appreciate how deep in the weeds you are if people don't feel empowered to speak up and provide critical feedback. Even if you are self-aware or open to feedback, your leadership habits may have been shaped by an autocratic boss in your past. Thus, your instincts are to control as much as possible, making it difficult to act on any information that speaks to the benefits of doing things differently.

Another problem presents when team members get the message that you don't trust them enough to get the job done. The problem becomes cyclical. If you don't trust them, they won't trust you.

Toxic cultures built on distrust make it even harder, if not impossible, to attract, retain, and develop the "A" players you need. Start by trusting your hiring process. Chapter 6 provides a detailed description of how to hire the "A" players you'll need. For now, let's discuss some options for creating an optimized culture.

CULTURAL MOTIVATORS

Once you've built a team of top talent, you need to continue using trust past the hiring process and embed it into your culture. This can be tricky because trust isn't necessarily a natural byproduct of the typical business. You must be the catalyst and make sure it sticks.

Perhaps you're open to learning more about the benefits of leading with trust but you need some evidence to solidify your buy-in. The books *Drive,* by Daniel Pink, and *Payoff,* by Dan Ariely, explore the most critical motivators for people in the workplace.

- Autonomy, ownership, and responsibility to create good work and generate strong feelings of accomplishment are fundamental motivators. (In my case, I wasn't providing those things to junior analysts early enough in my hedge fund career. I should have given them more room to generate investment ideas and see how they would perform.)
- People value challenging work, where they see an opportunity to make progress and accomplish something meaningful. They put in greater effort and value their roles more when they're doing more than just repetitive tasks all day. (When I handed off tasks to junior analysts, it was usually grunt work that I double-checked. I should have challenged them to improve their knowledge of stocks and portfolio analysis.)

- "A" players desire work with purpose. They want to feel a connection to something bigger than themselves. Often, the best work from team members comes when they can see they're making an impact.

Pink and Ariely's work shows these are bigger drivers of long-term motivation and fulfillment than extrinsic motivators like compensation. These motivators are the opposite of controlling team members' work, being deep in their weeds to spearhead everything, and leaving them with only unfulfilling scraps from your loaded plate of critical business issues.

To deliver on each of these key motivators, you must find ways to build trust and maintain it throughout your culture. Simply identifying it as a bylaw isn't enough to properly motivate people. You must take actionable steps that make trust come alive in the workplace.

TRUST BUILDERS

> "Before you are a leader, success is all about growing yourself. When you become a leader, success is all about growing others."
>
> —Jack Welch, former chairman and CEO of General Electric (GE)

The key to being able to trust your people is getting them to trust you. Think of it like a romantic relationship. If someone doesn't trust you to stay faithful, how can you trust them to do the same?

This is easier said than done. A study by the *Harvard Business Review* showed that 58 percent of team members trust a stranger more than their boss.[12] As terrifying as that sounds, it doesn't have to be that way.

Robin Dreek wrote one of the best books ever written about trust, called *The Code of Trust*. In it, he states that one of the best ways to earn others' trust is to be generous with your own trust. In other words, lead by example and show them you trust them!

LEADERSHIP CIRCLE OF TRUST
RYAN RENTERIA

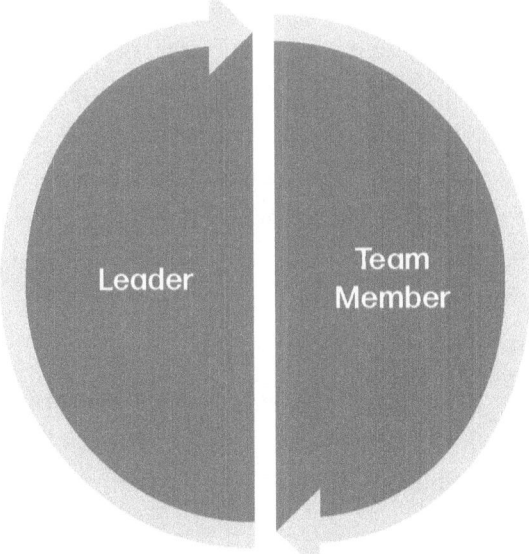

A leader has a profound impact on culture when they emulate the behavior they want from others. This runs parallel to Cialdini's reciprocation principle, which says that if you do a favor for someone (such as trusting them), they feel obligated to return it (such as trusting you), even if they don't like you!

With that said, what are some of the best ways to show team members you trust them?

Prove your dedication to the growth of your team members' careers by coaching them on how to be great leaders. Offer resources to help them solve their biggest problems. By lending your expertise in this way, you're showing people that you believe in them. You wouldn't waste your time if you didn't.

By doing whatever you can to help others achieve their goals, you gain their trust. People will notice when you genuinely care for their best interests. They will trust your intentions, your loyalty to them, and your selflessness to do what's right for the company.

Another way to build trust is to assume excellence and empower others with the autonomy to own higher-level tasks and more challenging work. "A" players especially want to feel a sense of accomplishment and know that they're growing their skill set. When you get out of the weeds, team members will feel more motivated and loyal from the deeper sense of purpose in their roles. The benefit for you is more time. You'll be able to block regular slots on your calendar for strategic thinking. Likewise, you'll have more time for work-life optimization.

Studies have shown that higher teacher expectations lead to stronger performance by students, which predicts greater overall academic achievement.[13] The same relationship holds true in the workplace.

Look at every major task on your plate and organize them into three buckets:

1. Items for which you can trust others to do the work and make a decision without your involvement. Say to them, "I trust you to make the best long-term decision for the company, so I'll respect whatever you decide."

2. Items for which you can trust others to do the work and bring you in for the last 10 percent to help make or approve the final decision. Tell them, "You can trust me to honor your hard work and expertise by truly listening to your recommendation and incorporating it into my decision matrix." If your decision goes in a different direction from what the team member was leaning toward, you can start by saying,

"I completely see your point of view and why you arrived there."

3. Items for which you should be deeply involved in the entire process. Over time, this list should become smaller. Even for the items that remain on your plate, you shouldn't be doing everything.

By creating these buckets, you systematize your trust-building with team members. This can be especially helpful if getting out of the minutiae doesn't come naturally to you.

Leaders often overlook the opportunity to show support when a team member's efforts result in a bad outcome. Instead of getting furious, you can tell them that you trust them and their positive intentions, so you want to focus more on how the team can learn from this situation and get better.

Punishing people only stresses them out, sends their minds racing, and distracts them from delivering peak performance; supporting them can lead to better results. People appreciate when you have their back.

Aside from being generous with your own trust, there are other ways to earn trust from team members.

Team members appreciate when you display intellectual honesty and hold yourself as accountable as you hold them. Bosses are wrong all the time. If you take a stance of denial or twist the facts to remain beyond reproach, team members will not trust you enough to admit their own mistakes. Rather, they'll attempt to cover them up or withhold information. In that case, you will have built a two-way culture of deceit.

"It takes twenty years to build a reputation and five minutes to ruin it."

—Warren Buffett, American business magnate, investor, and philanthropist

You must admit mistakes in order to model responsibility and vulnerability. Live what you're preaching and dispassionately dissect your own mistakes to improve future decisions versus using confirmation bias to support your narrative.

When apologizing is the right thing to do, just do it. Don't say you're sorry and then use the word "but" followed by an excuse, or even facts that led to the mistake.

In addition, displaying your own 360-degree feedback and asking others to hold you accountable will go far in earning their trust.

BEST PRACTICES FOR EFFECTIVE OFFSITES

Another great way to build a culture of two-way trust is through effective offsites. I've helped leaders plan offsites where team members build trust by getting to know each other on a personal level. An entire book could be written on the subject, but I'll provide a few of the best practices here.

Get feedback before anybody hits the road. Find out the top one to three things everyone thinks the team should focus on solving during the retreat. Then, circulate an agenda that states, "We want to extract and synthesize the group's collective expertise on issues X, Y, and Z to make great decisions."

Have everyone write potential solutions to the previously agreed-upon issues. To avoid groupthink, they should submit these views beforehand. Your goal during the retreat should be to come to a final decision on these issues through healthy dialogue.

A social activity the night before getting to business is a great way to loosen everybody up. This will make people more collaborative the next day. You could do something simple like dinner and drinks, or maybe something a little more unique like wine, beer, or chocolate tastings. Watching a sporting event is a good choice as well because it gets people to talk for an extended period of time.

Offsites are a good opportunity to have "get closer" activities where vulnerability breeds trust.

Start by having people tell fun facts about themselves. People can talk about unique expertise, favorite restaurants, volunteer activities, sports participation, or anything that comprises a big part

A few years ago, a CEO client asked me for help in planning their offsite for the executive leadership team. While their intentions were good, I noticed they had mapped out the entire event without asking the team for feedback. My client chose the specific issue to be addressed and even what direction they wanted to go on that issue.

I explained to my client that they were showing the team they did not trust them to have valuable input on decision-making. We worked together to change that.

They queried the team in advance to design the agenda together. The new goal was to have a healthy dialogue, collaboration, and trust to achieve unity in solving one key issue. By establishing the issue as a critical decision that required everyone's contributions, team members were more motivated to prepare in advance and actively engage in the dialogue. At the offsite, my client was blown away by the quality of ideas and level of participation from even the most reserved executives. The feedback he received about the offsite was amazing.

of who they are. This can facilitate common ground and generate rapport.

You can also have people talk about personal challenges, difficult events, or significant mistakes in their past.

Another related option is asking people to articulate their current workplace strengths and weaknesses. These exercises bring out everyone's vulnerability, which can be a foundational piece for trust among the entire group.

In addition to getting people to open up about themselves, it's also a good idea to allow everyone a chance to compliment others for specific skills or achievements in the workplace or thank others for help they've provided.

All these things lead to team members building connections as humans instead of simply coworkers. This makes the unhealthy type of conflict less likely in the workplace and encourages people to trust each other more.

When you're ready to start digging into the core issues on the agenda, start with a motivational message that aligns everyone, something like, "We have three thousand employees counting on us to solve hard problems together and make great long-term decisions for the company. The only way to do that is to create a trusted safe space to share here today. Each one of you must be respected because you all have valuable ideas to contribute and deserve to be heard. We must assume positive intent from each other."

At the conclusion of the offsite, someone should prepare a final document that lays out the action steps for the team to take and individual accountability. This way everyone knows to be rowing in the same direction, and they know what they're personally responsible for.

Offsite events are great for building team chemistry. I was fortunate enough to play a small role in an organization that had excellent team chemistry, and oddly enough, it began with an offsite... way offsite, in Asia.

TEAM CHEMISTRY

I saw how a culture with two-way trust excelled when I was an advisor for the Indiana Pacers. I was invited to travel with the team to Manila and Taipei for two preseason games against the Houston Rockets.

On the trip, Luis Scola, who was one of the smartest and most curious players in the league, asked me about endgame scenarios, opponent tendencies, and other strategies. I told him that I advise the coaching staff about those things before games and they decide what to communicate to the players. Scola told me that he preferred to get that information directly from me because he wanted to know detailed tendencies of who he was going to be guarding each game.

I asked the head coach, Frank Vogel, if I could give scouting analyses directly to Scola each game. Because Vogel epitomized the servant leader, he said he trusted me to provide that type of information to Luis.

Scola began implementing some of these strategies on the court and grew to trust me more. Luis told other players about how these analytics were helping him. Soon, four more players asked for my analysis of who they'd be guarding each night.

Eventually, Vogel had me fly in before every playoff series to present an analysis of the upcoming opponent to the coaching staff. I also sat down with Scola and the four other players to discuss deeper analysis of the likely two or three players they were going to guard in the series.

Trust was on display in that scenario, and it started from the top. By giving me the autonomy to own challenging work, Frank Vogel showed trust in me, so others on the team did as well. Consequently, I trusted that they valued and considered the recommendations in their decisions. I also felt motivated to work even harder to provide the most differentiated analysis I could to the coaching staff and the team. My work felt more meaningful because I heard it was having a positive impact, even if I was just one of many team members playing a small role. By trusting me, Vogel gave me something far better than a pay raise: He gave me the chance to have meaning and contribute to something bigger than myself, which drove tremendous loyalty to the organization.

My excitement for the job grew even bigger when I got a surprise email from Scola while on vacation in Nantucket. This happened in early September, which is typically the last part of the only light time of year for the NBA. The draft happens in June. Free agents are signed in July and training camps don't happen until late September.

Scola's email said he was guarding Gorgui Dieng in the World Championships in Spain the next night. He wanted to know if I could send him analytics on Dieng. I was thrilled to jump off my chair on the beach, walk back to our house, and send Scola what he was looking for as soon as possible.

The two-way trust the organization had established worked well for everybody and led to solid team chemistry. The players got every resource they wanted to maximize performance. I felt more excited about my role, and the leader, Frank Vogel, scaled the business beyond himself. By empowering me to communicate opponent tendencies to whichever players wanted them, he ended up with more time to focus on building strategy.

Imagine the feeling you could give team members if you trusted them in this way. What kind of loyalty and talent retention would that generate? As a result, how much free time would open up on your schedule for strategic thinking?

Now that we've established trust as being critical to building a lead-without-burnout culture, how do you maximize it for the company's benefit? In the next chapter, you'll see how candor works as another foundational piece.

LEAD WITHOUT BURNOUT

▶ You need to get out of the weeds and spend more time on strategic thinking to better position your business for scalable growth and success.

▶ Understand the real motivators for employees and that trust is the most important factor to make each come to fruition.

▶ Establish a two-way culture of trust with your team. Trust them so they trust you, model the intellectual honesty you want to see, and conduct effective offsites where the team grows closer.

CHAPTER 4

CANDOR

"And unlike Lieutenant Kaffee, I actually can handle the truth."

—Ted Lasso, fictional soccer coach and
eternally optimistic servant leader

usiness leaders want to drive improved results through clearer and better-informed decision-making. The path to get there is with a culture that promotes continuous learning and growth for yourself, your team members, and the organization.

Old habits die hard and those that have built a level of success die even harder. You might not be accustomed to responding to critical feedback. If everyone around you has developed their own habits of telling you what they think you want to hear all the time, you won't be familiar with listening to oppositional views. Perhaps you give others' opinions a cursory nod of approval, but don't follow through on incorporating them into your leadership style. Another option is flat-out denial. Most likely, that's not you. If it was, you probably wouldn't have picked up this book.

If you're not actively seeking the opinions of others and incorporating them into your evolving leadership style, you're not modeling curiosity, continuous learning, and growth. This creates the antithesis of the culture you're seeking. Teammates won't seek out, truly hear, and incorporate feedback to improve their own processes when you aren't setting that example.

Unfortunately, most workplaces live in this space—one where few people want to engage in candor with leaders or coworkers. This is the worst-case scenario. It's time to overcome this serious obstacle to growth with candor. By implementing candor, you create a culture that improves learning, decision quality, and employee engagement.

SET THE TONE

Curiosity sets the tone for a high candor culture. In my experience, cultures that foster curiosity encourage employees to seek the truth and make intellectually honest decisions. Aside from leading to more candor, curiosity also helps employees to engage more deeply in their work, generate new ideas, and share innovation with others.[14]

Unfortunately, a disconnect exists between employers and employees around how much curiosity is encouraged in the workplace. A robust 83 percent of today's executives proudly state that they encourage curiosity, while only 52 percent of employees agree with them.

Having the curiosity and candor to seek intellectually honest answers is also critical to sound decision-making. Alarmingly, business leaders attribute only about 50 percent of their decisions to hard data, while the other half is credited to the processes and dynamics of the strategy room.[15] Given all the cognitive biases, politics, and personalities influencing the strategy room, it is crucial to set the tone for high candor to make dispassionate, evidence-based decisions.

Establish clear principles relating to candor as a cultural bylaw. These should be written on the first page of every meeting agenda and frequently reiterated at the outset of meetings. Here are some examples of candor principles you can share with your team.

You could say, "It is our duty to our employees, customers, suppliers, and investors to have truthful feedback and open debate." This contributes to your "A" players' desire for connection and commitment to something bigger than themselves.

A fundamental truth about human nature is that we want to be heard. People will "quiet quit" an emotional relationship when they feel ignored or not understood, and it is no different in the workplace. Tell team members that everyone is responsible for fostering an environment where people feel listened to and respected, not only by leadership but by each other as well. This will make your talented team members less likely to "quiet quit" or leave altogether.

Some team members may be reluctant to speak up if they're new to the organization or if this subject matter is not their area of expertise. Nobody wants to look foolish. Encourage team members to be patient and respectful so that everyone feels safe and comfortable making comments, even ones that may show their inexperience.

Everyone must trust that their colleagues have good intentions and the company's best long-term interests in mind. Assuming positive intent is powerful and contagious! With that in mind, everyone should expect that others will disagree with their ideas and may present counterpoints in a respectful way to foster a healthy debate. You should encourage people to play devil's advocate to your points as much as anyone else's. Similarly, team members should expect you to do the same with them. Intellectual honesty for the team is far more important than any individual being right.

Ensure everyone knows that no topic should be off-limits to open discussion, not even those that are against your or their personal interests. Anything that could be considered awkward or anxiety-inducing should not only be permitted, but championed! Good news is fun to share, but bad news is crucial to discuss. Contrarian views should be welcomed because they go against the grain and limit the risks associated with groupthink.

By praising the courage of others to bring up bad news or contribute opposing viewpoints, you trigger social proof. Cialdini's research found that people are more likely to do something when they see others doing it.

A workplace where people use candor to openly discuss anything is a sign of an organization with a growth mindset whose people care more about the team's improvement and long-term success than being right.

If you consistently show that you'll act on bad news and consider contrarian views, people will feel good about bringing them up. How confident are you that everyone on your team is comfortable proactively presenting bad news without spin and articulating ideas that might go against your views?

> *"Sometimes, I think my most important job as a CEO is to listen for bad news. If you don't act on it, your people will eventually stop bringing bad news to your attention and that is the beginning of the end."*
>
> —Bill Gates, cofounder of Microsoft

CREATING HIGH CANDOR IN GROUP MEETINGS

After setting the tone, ensure high candor is being welcomed and encouraged in all meetings. One way to facilitate that is to have all participants reflect on the most vital strengths, weaknesses, opportunities, and threats (SWOT) of the company, and provide thoughts on particular issues *before* the meeting. Tell people, "Come to the meeting ready to enlighten me and other members of the leadership team with thoughts on these topics. Challenge us with any questions about why we're doing XYZ instead of ABC. We don't have all the answers and we want to learn from you." When everyone has sent their responses, have someone on the leadership team review and prioritize them on the agenda by the most urgent or common themes.

Before the meeting, you should also assign a facilitator to ensure the high-candor principles are properly adhered to. Rotate this job after each meeting, and emphasize that facilitating dialogue and resolving workplace conflict are desirable skills to add to their experience. People should be excited when it is their turn to act as the candor facilitator. Also, avoid making yourself the facilitator, as participants are likely to act differently in that case.

Contrarian views should be encouraged during the meeting, and presenters from both sides of the issue must convey their views respectfully. This isn't always intuitive, as people from opposing sides of a debate have a tendency to become defensive or even argumentative. The tone can often turn snarky or condescending, causing the other side to feel personally attacked and shut down. If this happens, the facilitator should lower the temperature by reminding attendees that everyone has good intentions and that conflict is healthy for growth when it is done respectfully.

Details of each viewpoint should be fully fleshed out, rather than rushed through. If people feel hurried or invalidated in a different way, that makes them feel unheard. Candor cannot be a formality; it must be a genuine form of respectful two-way communication.

Post-meeting, the facilitators should develop follow-up action plans to ensure that whatever was discussed in the meeting gets implemented by the appropriate individuals. The facilitator must ensure these individuals are held accountable.

The result of driving group meetings with candor is that people will feel empowered to contribute more. Knowing they can speak freely and will be heard, even if they have a different opinion from leadership, is an invaluable perk in any workplace.

An example I've seen of this from my own experience occurred when I was an advisor for the Indiana Pacers.

We flew to Cleveland for a playoff series against the Lebron James-led Cavaliers. Our GM, Kevin Pritchard, invited me to dinner with him, Larry Bird, who was our president of basketball operations, and our VP of basketball ops, Peter Dinwiddie. I knew we'd chat about potential additions to our roster with the draft and free agency looming in the coming months, so I needed to come prepared.

Most people know that Larry Bird is a basketball legend (his nickname is actually "Larry Legend"). Fewer know that he is the only person in the history of professional sports to be named Most Valuable Player, Front Office Executive of the Year (GM), and Coach of the Year. That feat seems unlikely to be accomplished by anyone again for a long time.

Sure, the team's owner hired me to provide advice to the front office, but obviously Larry knows infinitely more about basketball than I will ever know. It would have been reasonable for him to dismiss my opinions.

Over the course of the dinner discussion, we all chimed in with our opinions about prospects in the upcoming NBA draft. I was hesitant to bring up certain players I liked who looked better on analytics than through the traditional basketball lens.

I finally decided to share these contrarian ideas and why I liked these players. As it turned out, Larry listened respectfully and made me feel heard. I felt safe and motivated to contribute whatever I could to this high-candor dialogue because Larry's leadership showed he knew I had good intentions and was just trying to help the Pacers. I felt an incredible sense of purpose and meaning in my role coming out of that evening.

Larry has always been considered an elite leader in NBA circles, and that became even more clear to me that night. On a night when I could have been made to feel ignored or dismissed, I felt like an appreciated member of the team. Let's be frank: I knew the leadership group would receive opinions from several team members and didn't know to what extent they would consider or weigh each. Nonetheless, what an experience that night was! It motivated me to be curious, work even harder to pursue unconventional ideas, and speak up knowing that they wouldn't be immediately dismissed.

Some of your teammates may see you as a legend with significantly more experience and knowledge. When you practice high-candor principles as a leader, you'll motivate them to speak up with potentially valuable ideas.

> *"I try to have young people around me who are not afraid to speak their mind to me and argue with me. If somebody's here too long and they agree with everything I say, they're not here too much longer."*
>
> —Stanley Druckenmiller, legendary
> investor and hedge fund manager

CHOOSE OPEN-ENDED QUESTIONS OVER DEFINITIVE STATEMENTS

You want to avoid making definitive statements about issues—something like, "Well, this acquisition target is clearly a great fit if we can get it at the right price." That stops the conversation. In that case, you're telling people the answer and squashing their motivation to offer any differing opinions that may provide valuable insight. Instead, ask open-ended questions that spark curiosity.

- What do you think of this?
- What ideas do you have for attacking this?
- Can you explain your perspective a bit more and what's causing you to have that perspective?
- What are some of the biggest positives of taking this approach?
- What about this approach doesn't sit well with you?
- What are the biggest challenges you face in solving this and what are some things I could do to help you alleviate those challenges?
- If you had unlimited resources, how would you attack this issue?
- If you had 100 percent decision-making authority, what would you do?

When you were in the shoes of one of your team members and raised a point to your boss and they countered with a definitive statement, did it make you feel empowered to stand by your point or speak up again when a different issue arose? Almost certainly not. Definitive statements close the discussion. Open-ended questions inspire creativity, innovation, and growth.

"I only wish I could find an institute that teaches people how to listen. Business people need to listen at least as much as they need to talk. Too many people fail to realize that real communication goes in both directions."

—Lee Iacocca, former CEO of Chrysler Corporation

WHAT ABOUT THE GORILLA IN THE ROOM?

I once gave a speech to a room full of hedge fund managers where I played a two-minute video of something called the Monkey Business Illusion. The video was created by experimental psychologist and cognitive scientist Daniel Simons. It's under two minutes long and it shows six people dribbling basketballs. The narrator asks the viewer to track the number of times the three people dressed in white shirts pass the ball. In the middle of the video, a gorilla walks into the room, one of the players wearing a black shirt leaves, and the curtain in the background changes color.

According to Simons, most people can correctly answer that the players wearing white shirts passed the ball sixteen times. But only half of them notice that a person in a gorilla suit walks into the middle of the room, pounds their chest a few times, and exits the other side.

What's the point of the video? It's impossible to apply the same level of focus to two or more things at a time that you can when just one target demands your attention. I played that video because I wanted people to realize that it's difficult, at best, to truly listen to their fellow team members if they're constantly thinking of counterarguments while the other person is talking.

"Most people do not listen with the intent to understand, they listen with the intent to reply."

—Steven Covey

A serious communication breakdown occurs if you don't actually listen to others when they're engaging you in conversation. Not only do you not get the benefit of their viewpoint, but you're more likely to interrupt and correct them.

When you focus on listening instead of thinking of your counterarguments, you acquire the value of their input and validate their contributions. Both participants get something out of that situation.

After you've listened to the other person's point of view, start by repeating their idea back to them: "It sounds like you're saying XYZ." Further validate it with something along the lines of, "That's a great point that I didn't fully appreciate. It makes a lot of sense because of A, B, and C. Let me research it further and see if we can incorporate your point into our decision process."

When you're ready to offer your own opinion, you can lower the odds of a defensive response or the risk of making the person feel unheard. Say something like, "I could definitely be wrong here and please tell me if I'm missing something…" or, "Feel free to rip this apart, but I think there are merits to considering X, Y, and Z. Here's why…"

After further research and thought, you might decide to make an adjustment on one or more aspects of the issue because of what the other person said. If so, you can make them feel tremendously valued by saying some version of, "I want to show you how your points influenced my decision process. I have a lot of respect for your opinion, so I'm going to make XYZ adjustments. Maybe you and I can follow this closely to see how it starts to play out. Thank you so much for bringing this insight to my attention."

GIVING FEEDBACK

If an outcome goes sideways for a team member, they're likely to be pretty hard on themselves. That's part of most "A" players' personalities. One of the goals of your meeting should be to quickly get this valuable member of your team back into a good headspace where they can operate at peak performance again.

First, objectively determine if the undesirable outcome was the result of a mistake in the team member's process or if something happened that was out of their control. Regardless of that conclusion, start the interaction with empathy by letting the person know you care about them and you believe in them. Tell them that you know they have positive intent and always try to do what is best for the company. Skipping this introduction could demolish all the other demonstrations of high candor you've established, at least in this person's mind. You need to focus on empathy and find common ground.

If the outcome was beyond their control, empathize and offer assistance: "Sorry you're feeling XYZ emotions. I get it because a similar situation happened to me when I was in your position and I felt the same way. This was a bad break, but I know you'll get past it just like I did because I believe in you and your process. In hindsight, I wouldn't be where I am today if I didn't learn to quickly move on from the mental hangups caused by outcomes just like this one. Now, how can I help you to get past this?"

When the outcome was due to a mistake, try something like, "Hey, I know I've made plenty of mistakes in my career. I expect you to make them too. Are you open to making improvements to this part of your process one of your biggest areas of focus? Yes? Great! Here are a few ways that I think can help you with that. Now, is there anything else you feel I can do to help you with this?"

In either case, focus on the action, not the person. If they feel you're thinking negatively about them, they'll feel more negative about themselves, lose confidence, and struggle to return to peak performance.

Whether the meeting was about a mistake or a bad break, always close the conversation with something reinforcing and motivational that lets them know how valued they are: "I'm telling you this because your skill set and quality of work are impressive. I think you're going to be one of the important stars to take this company to the next level. I'm not sure you even fully appreciate your upside, but I see zero limits to your growth and potential for impact. I care deeply about helping you get there and this is one of the ways I can show it."

> *"You lead by letting others know what you expect of them, which may exceed what they themselves expect. Provide them a reputation that they can step up to."*
>
> —**Kevin Kelly,** *Excellent Advice for Living*

When I worked for the Pacers, I benefited tremendously from feedback in a one-on-one setting with Nate McMillan, who was the head coach at the time.

I emailed the coaching staff and front office an analysis of our team's performance the previous night. My intentions were good. I wanted to provide helpful information that showed we didn't take advantage of our opponent's biggest weakness. But the way I communicated it was terrible. I don't remember exactly what I said, but my words were not articulated with the level of respect, empathy, or humility that they should have been. They violated some of the principles for candor that were mentioned earlier.

I happened to be in Indianapolis that day, and Nate called me into his office shortly after he received the email. When I started walking down the long hall toward his office, I realized I had made an ignorant mistake. Suddenly, the words I had written rang a little differently in my head. I started to realize that I should have been more careful in my communication, and now I figured the head coach was going to rip me apart about it.

When I walked in, Nate said, "Look, I know you're just trying to do your job, but how does this type of communication help us to achieve our goals? How could you write it better to help us get to where we want to be?" Coach McMillan blew me away with his amazingly thoughtful and purposeful leadership.

Notice how he started his talk by empathizing with me and acknowledging my positive intent to the organization: "I know you're just trying to do your job..." Rather than tearing my head off or making definitive statements, he empathized and asked me open-ended questions to help me get better at my job. This is the epitome of a successful high-candor culture. It is also one of many reasons Nate McMillan is one of the winningest coaches in NBA history and is held in high regard by countless owners, executives, and players.

ASK FOR FEEDBACK ON YOUR PERFORMANCE

Leaders who ranked in the top 10 percent in asking for feedback were rated, on average, at the 86th percentile in overall leadership effectiveness.[16]

You need to schedule separate one-on-ones, where the sole purpose is to ask for feedback on your performance. You cannot review a team member's performance and have them review yours in the same session. There's too much at stake for the person you're evaluating. Inevitably, your feedback will be watered down or de-emphasized in that scenario. Especially if someone's bonus or pay raise is at stake, they're not likely to provide you with a genuine opinion of your performance.

Consider some of the following sample questions as solid prompts for soliciting feedback in these dedicated meetings.

- What do you think I'm doing well and why?
- What could I be doing better?
- Why do you think I'm struggling with those things?
- Do you have any ideas for how I could improve in those areas?
- How can I help make your life better and easier?

Take plenty of handwritten notes when people deliver the candor for which you're looking. This shows people you're actively listening and respect what they have to say.

Another great way to personify the candor you want in your culture is when they're highlighting a mistake that you've made or a problem that you've played a role in creating. Instead of getting defensive, own the results. Boldly show accountability by admitting your mistakes and sincerely apologizing for them when you feel it's necessary. No "buts" are allowed in an apology. A "but" is a precursor to an excuse, and that can weaken authenticity. The last time you told your significant other, "I'm sorry, but…," how did that go?

By having the candor to sincerely admit fault, you're modeling for team members to do the same rather than cover up problems. They will realize that you'll treat their failures and shortcomings with empathy, not volatility, as long as they own them. Accountability maximizes your credibility. It also enhances the odds of future high-candor discussions, which are critical for using mistakes as opportunities to get better.

Displaying such vulnerability can be difficult for anyone. Think of it this way: Which is better for the growth of the organization, modeling intellectual honesty or being beyond reproach by sheer title or status?

Tell the person you're going to come up with action steps to address the opportunities for improvement they've alerted you to. When you have time to create several actionable steps, write them down on your to-do list, show them to whoever gave you the feedback, and ask them to hold you accountable for following through.

> *"Winning isn't anything you own. You just rent it, and then you have to pay the rent daily."*
> **—Stan Moss, CEO of Polen Capital**

Most people will be shocked at this level of candor. Team members don't expect such humility from leadership on a regular basis, so keep the momentum going when you build that candor. This will also make people more likely to display the same level of humility and candor when working with others and you. Another benefit is that this leadership is conducive to building loyalty throughout your organization. People won't want to leave when they feel heard, respected, and trusted. Candor diminishes the odds of quiet quitting or people looking for another job.

If you show your employees you can handle the truth, imagine the improvement in the team's growth, decision-making, and results. Also, imagine how much more employees will feel empowered, and how much your load will be lightened to free up time for strategic thinking and work-life optimization.

You now understand how trust and candor contribute to a more productive and more appreciated workplace. But how can we ask our team members to trust and be open with each other unless we become creative, innovative, and best-in-class at bolstering their mental health?

LEAD WITHOUT BURNOUT

▶ Set the tone for high candor at the top of every meeting agenda and at the beginning of every meeting.

▶ Take the necessary steps to ensure high candor permeates group and one-on-one meetings.

▶ Asking for feedback on your performance is a highly effective way to encourage candor in your positive culture.

CHAPTER 5

MENTAL HEALTH

"The pandemic has cast a spotlight on the need to address mental health in the workplace. As business leaders, we have a responsibility to break down the stigma associated with mental health issues like stress and anxiety to ensure everyone can thrive at work."

—Punit Renjen, global CEO emeritus of Deloitte

It's time for me to walk the talk. Over the first four chapters, I've preached a different kind of leadership gospel concerning balance, cultural bylaws, trust, and candor. To open this crucial chapter about the importance of supporting strong mental health in the workplace, it's only fitting that I share my experience with anxiety in my own life. Some of it may sound familiar. Even if it doesn't, understand that a startlingly high percentage of your team members may have similar struggles. Many of them might be the strongest "A" players in your company. After reading my story and the principles to promote strong mental health in this chapter, you'll be equipped to help yourself and others to achieve optimal mental health.

I lived with anxiety for the first forty-two years of my life. Most of the time, it was mild, but occasionally, it was overwhelming.

Anxiety probably first manifested for me in my earliest years, when often I witnessed my parents fighting. They ultimately divorced while I was still young. I'm grateful I was able to maintain a relationship with my father, who taught me a lot about work ethic, but my mom had primary custody and was a superstar. She raised me as a single mom and kindergarten teacher in a lower-middle-class household in Sacramento, California.

Mom was determined to save every penny she could for my college fund, so she bought only the bare necessities. I wore mostly hand-me-down clothes from the older kids of her fellow teachers. We rarely went out to eat and couldn't afford air conditioning even with the 100+ degree days of Sacramento summers. The public high school I attended got shut down for bad test scores, a high dropout rate, and an extensive history of campus violence.

We knew many people had it much worse than us, though. Thankfully, we never feared going without food or shelter. Due to my mom's immense strength and gracious nature, she also spent countless hours volunteering to help others who were in extremely difficult economic situations.

Nonetheless, a constant deep anxiety about our financial situation loomed over us. Mom was an absolute rock star, but that financial pressure heightened her lifelong generalized anxiety. I'm sure I inherited some anxiety from her. When you feel financial stress as a kid, it doesn't go away as an adult. It stays with you almost regardless of how much money you make, because you irrationally fear you can lose your resources at any time and revert to that difficult situation.

Later in life, I felt tremendous guilt for even having such anxiety about first-world problems. My brain rationally knew that no matter what happened, I'd be fine financially. I became furious at myself for even having these worrisome thoughts when others had much bigger problems. People were battling disease, starvation, and horrible atrocities every day, and I was spinning my wheels about picking the right stock.

Many years of cognitive behavioral therapy (CBT) helped bring clarity to my situation. I finally understood that no matter how confident I was in my abilities or how successful I became professionally, part of me was having irrational thoughts about the future. I would create "what if" scenarios and catastrophize them by assuming the worst case. "What if this investment turns out to be a dud? I'll probably get fired." I would also play mind reader. "Why hasn't the head coach responded to my text from this morning? He's probably upset at the analysis I wrote about our team."

It didn't matter that I understood these thoughts and feelings to be completely irrational. They still kept me awake for good starting at 3:00 or 4:00 a.m., making my days stressful and exhausting. I was constantly on edge and sometimes had a short fuse with others. My anxiety made it difficult to be truly present and enjoy my time with friends and family away from work.

I am deeply grateful for finally overcoming anxiety after many years of working on it. CBT taught me several impactful strategies to manage my problem. Now, I'm sharing them, hoping that they can have a similarly positive effect on you or someone you know. It's especially helpful if you journal these an hour or two before bed because that action reduces the odds of your mind racing after waking up in the middle of the night.

- Ask yourself, "What's the worst that can happen?" Will that completely destroy you, or will you recover? Are you overestimating the odds of the worst case? What is the most likely alternative outcome that is more of a middle ground? Are you underestimating your ability to handle the situation? You will probably be OK no matter what.

- Normalize the anxiety. Know that many other high achievers experience the same thoughts, concerns, and fears. According to the World Health Organization, one in eight people worldwide lives with a mental disorder.[17] The prevalence of mental health conditions is notably higher among CEOs, with 49 percent experiencing issues.[18] Celebrities including Oprah, Stephen Colbert, Jonah Hill, Emma Stone, Ryan Reynolds, Michael Phelps, Kevin Love, Demar Derozan, and many executives have spoken publicly about anxiety and other mental health issues. Give yourself the grace to shed your guilt. Know that it's OK to experience these thoughts even if others in the world are experiencing more acute problems. Your feelings are real and worthy.

- For whatever part of the situation that is in your control, write an action plan to deal with it. Then, you know that you have done everything possible to prepare to do the best job. The rest is largely out of your control. It's pointless to get upset with yourself for something out of your control.

- I developed the following realization on my own, and it has perhaps been the most powerful strategy of all for me. Put aside professional outcomes. By waking up every day and approaching things in a kind, honest, and high-integrity manner, you can slash your anxiety because you have done everything in your control to do the right thing.

I expose myself in this section not solely to help other business leaders who have experienced anxiety. If you've been fortunate enough to avoid this, I hope this section gives you an appreciation for the impact mental health issues could be having on your teammates, even those who appear most successful from the outside.

Prioritize mental health in the workplace and understand how big a role you can play in helping everyone to work and live with less anxiety. It takes a lot of grace and empathy to do this, but it is perhaps the most crucial aspect of leading without burnout for yourself and your team members.

To fully execute on this, you must also ensure the leaders and managers below you learn the principles covered in this chapter, so it permeates throughout the organization.

The numbers tell us that mental health is a top priority for team members seeking a cultural fit for their skills.

- 75 percent of team members have experienced burnout at work.[19]
- 80 percent of team members would quit a job over mental health.[20]
- 73 percent of team members and 81 percent of managers indicated they would be more likely to stay at a company that offered high-quality mental health resources.[21]
- Team members who feel supported by their employers are 45 percent less likely to experience mental health symptoms and 5.6 times more likely to trust their employers.[22]

I've seen these numbers play out in my coaching. One of the top concerns I hear from my CEO clients is about team member burnout and how they can help reduce the risk. One of them recently requested we make reducing burnout for his nearly five thousand employees a top focus of our work this year. Imagine the purpose and meaning he'll feel as he executes on that!

Today's younger generations of top talent have choices and priorities that previous top-tier talent didn't have. If you're going to attract, retain, and develop the best people, you must execute mental health in your culture in ways that go beyond traditional benefits.

Start with a high level of caring for your people, not just because it will enable them to perform at their best and foster strong loyalty, but also because it's the right thing to do. Genuinely caring for

others is tremendously fulfilling and there is nothing more important in life.

CARING

At a young age, I learned everything I needed to know about caring from my mother. Remembering the way she cared for each
individual she volunteered to help, even when she was struggling
to make ends meet in her own household, inspired me to leave
Wall St. at a young age and work exclusively as a volunteer with
disadvantaged children for two years.

That experience was not entirely a selfless act. Because I got in the
trenches and got to know the kids versus serving on a board or
fundraising (which are also important), the kids developed tight
bonds with me. It was an incredibly rewarding experience. I received confirmation of all the research that shows how helping
others leads to your own increased well-being.

> *"Perhaps the most counterintuitive truth of the universe is that
> the more you give to others, the more you'll get. Understanding
> this is the beginning of wisdom."*
>
> —Kevin Kelly, *Excellent Advice for Living*

Today, I lean on that caring to help my executive coaching clients.
As a result, nearly all of them have stayed with me long-term. Some
of the most consistent areas I focus on with them are: developing
deeper relationships with their team members, investing heavily in
a culture that promotes strong mental health, and optimizing their
own work-life balance. Whenever a client comes back to me with
positive results from this approach, or acknowledges how deeply
I care about them, I get the added benefit of increasing my own
well-being. That's why I chose to do this over other endeavors.

As a leader, you deal with stressors that most people don't have, but your team members have issues that affect them just as significantly. They may not be as fortunate as you with regard to freedom of their schedule or economic status. Many of them have sick family members or their own mental or physical sickness with which to deal. Some team members have relationship troubles, parenting issues, or financial burdens. All of these things can put massive amounts of pressure on anyone. When you show that you care deeply about them, you not only help them to deal with their problems better, you also increase their loyalty. Another byproduct is that those you care about will pay it forward to other leaders, team members, and families.

One way to show people you care is to display your humanity. Chat about nonwork-related topics to deepen connections. San Antonio Spurs head coach Greg Popovich has made it a point throughout his career to get to know his players on as deep a level as possible. Furthermore, he encourages his players to embrace their humanity. One of his former players, Will Perdue, has said, "I was kind of amazed by how much he wanted to know about you as an individual." Other coaches stopped short of where Popovich was willing to go. "They cared about you, but they didn't really want to overextend themselves in case you got cut or traded…I don't think Pop ever even considered that. He saw you as a human being first and a basketball player second."[23]

While engaging in casual conversation, ask team members about their bigger-picture personal dreams and goals. Find out what their challenges are in life and see if you can offer some insight that might help them. Keep in mind that serving as a supportive sounding board rather than concentrating on direct advice may be better for everyone.

During my days on Wall Street, Michael Karsch always showed a deep level of caring in his leadership style. He knew that I cared a great deal about my next-door neighbor from my childhood home, Elizabeth Daily. She watched me while my parents were at work and became like a second mother to me. Actually, "Lizzie D" ended up creating a full daycare, where she also watched about eight other kids every day for nearly thirty years. Uncertainty over her health developed while I worked for Michael. By talking to me as a human, not as a hedge fund manager, he knew that she was one of the most important people in the world to me. When she got sick, he helped me to try to find the best medical care possible for her. That showed me how deeply he cared about me as a person.

Michael also knew I cared a lot about certain charitable foundations. Unfortunately, my job there dictated that there was no time for me to spend engaging in volunteer activities. Instead, I focused on making financial contributions. Michael happily made generous donations to charities I supported while I worked at his company.

By virtue of these acts of caring, I developed supreme loyalty to Michael. I got calls from recruiters all the time while I worked for him, but I turned them down. Nothing they could offer me was worth the relationship he had forged with me.

That level of caring from leadership also inspired my analysis of investment opportunities. While investigating companies, I always tried to reach out to former employees and ask them how they felt about the leadership situation. Specifically, I would ask them, "Do you feel like the CEO cares deeply about their individual team members?" Incidentally, the names that always arose as favorable were Jim Sinegal of Costco and Greg Henslee of O'Reilly Automotive, and it is no surprise those stocks crushed the S&P 500 during their leadership.

Another form of caring is regularly checking in with team members about work topics. See if there's anything you can do to help them with specific problems such as investing in a resource for them or reducing their bureaucracy. Ask them about their professional goals and dreams and how you can help them get there. As Cialdini's reciprocity principle teaches us, they'll be more motivated to help you overcome problems and reach your growth ambitions.

EMPATHY

Although caring to connect with people on a human level is key to attracting and retaining "A" players, you should be cautious about giving definitive advice. Regardless of the situation, however, empathy is always a welcome trait among leadership and colleagues.

A Management Research Group study found empathy to be the most important competence for effective leadership. Yet the global leadership consulting firm DDI found that only 40 percent of leaders have basic empathy skills.

In its Empathy in Business Survey, Ernst & Young discovered that 90 percent of team members believe empathetic leadership leads to greater job satisfaction, while 79 percent think it lowers turnover. An overwhelming 85 percent see empathetic bosses as having an effect on increased productivity among employees.[24]

These numbers speak to the critical nature of empathy in the culture you build and maintain. There is a science behind it, which I learned a lot about while training for 7 Cups, a website that offers empathetic listening for people who need it. I signed up to be a volunteer listener with them and followed their techniques to engage in conversations with over 500 people who were struggling with mental health challenges including depression, anxiety, and suicidal thoughts. I have also given speeches on the powerful fundamentals of empathy and communication to hedge fund leaders who operate in a ruthless industry. If they can learn how to empathize, you certainly can! The following are some examples of how to engage someone who could use a little empathy in their day:

- So sorry to hear you're experiencing that (emotion).
- Tell me more about that.
- I can see why you'd feel that way. I've been there too.
- No wonder you're frustrated. I'd feel the same way.
- I appreciate you opening up to me about that.

Another way to show empathy is by asking questions (not giving advice) like the following:

- What is the most important thing you want the person to understand?
- What, in your mind, needs to change?
- What would you say to a friend if they were in your situation?
- How can I best support you right now? (This is also one of the best questions you can ever ask your children. Try it!)

You can also try to champion the person with specific, positive feedback and encouragement.

- You're handling things really well. I'm not sure if I would be able to do the same if I were in your shoes.
- That's a good idea/suggestion you came up with; I'm impressed with X.
- Affirm it's their choice and support/respect whatever they decide.

Finally, there may be no greater source of empathy than sharing your own similar experience. An example of that would be, "I don't want to give you any direct advice, especially without knowing the details as intimately as you. As long as you accept what I have to say as just one person's experience I'll share what's worked for me and others I know."

Have you ever had a boss show empathy in one of these ways? If so, how fondly do you remember them?

RECOGNITION

Caring and empathy add to the happiness of the giver and the receiver. In that way, they're fantastic for the overall mental health of you and your team members. They're also great motivators, as they contribute to loyalty and make people want to perform at their best. Recognition of achievement and gestures of gratitude are also excellent contributors to strong mental health, especially in front of others. Never underestimate the power of flattery.

In his best-seller *Payoff*, Dan Ariely proved the power of compliments in the workplace. His study showed a group that received a compliment from their boss outperformed a group that received monetary rewards.

A Cialdini reciprocity study takes Ariely's work a step further, noting that the effect of nice gestures scales when a surprise factor is involved. Think of it as the same idea that's worked so well for great brands in the hospitality industry—delight customers by surprising them.

Yes, you can delight your team members by surprising them with compliments and gestures of gratitude as well. The only prerequisites are that your words must be authentic and geared toward their specific achievements or strengths. You must also follow through with actions consistent with those words. Specific surprise compliments and genuine gestures of gratitude are some of the most powerful leadership actions you can take to bolster mental health, productivity, and loyalty.

A particularly impactful experience with recognition happened for me in my NBA analytics days. Frank Vogel surprised me with a text one day, saying that I was an invaluable part of the team's success because of how I analyzed and communicated opponents' tendencies.

Frank is known to be a positive coach who gives a lot of encouraging feedback, but this was still unexpected and more specific than "good job," so I appreciated it. His carefully chosen words contributed to my mental health by making me feel good about my contributions to the team. Still, there was a little piece of me that wondered how real his sentiment was. He answered that doubt with how he followed through in our next conversation. He told me that he wanted me to fly out before every playoff series to present to the coaching staff in person, so they would get an even greater understanding of the opponent's tendencies before they planned practices and strategies for the series.

He went on to say that if the team won a third game of a series, he wanted me to fly out to meet them wherever they were. If they went on to win a clinching game, he wanted me to be able to meet with them soon after to talk about the next series.

After a series-clinching win in Washington, D.C., led by David West's gutsy performance, I said to David in the locker room, "We didn't need to know a damn thing about Washington's analytical tendencies with how dominant you were tonight."

After the plane ride back to Indiana, I met Frank in his office. He held up my slides about the Washington series and said, "The last series all started here (pointing to a specific analysis on one slide). Now, let's get ready for the Miami Heat and see what you have for me."

Let's be clear: I knew I was just one of many in our organization who helped contribute in a small way, but the way Frank once again checked all the boxes of effective recognition as a leader—surprise, authenticity, specificity, and follow-through—was massively beneficial to my motivation and mental health.

How often are you highlighting your team members' best accomplishments in individual and group meetings by including all those components of recognition? Try it more often. Encourage them to shower each other with surprising, authentic, specific recognition as well.

THANK YOU

Recognizing your team members' value and achievements can be enhanced by starting with two simple words: thank you!

A recent study by Workhuman unveiled some interesting facts surrounding workers who are thanked and recognized for their contributions.

- They are roughly half as likely to look for a new job (26 percent versus 49 percent).
- They are twice as likely to be highly engaged at work (60 percent versus 32 percent).
- They are three times more likely to consider their work meaningful and purposeful (53 percent versus 18 percent).
- A much greater number of them also report being happier at work (47 percent versus 11 percent).[25]

When you want to recognize employees by showing your appreciation for their quality work, expert insight, or other efforts, handwritten notes are even more impactful than typed emails because they show a deeper level of care. However, the act of recognition can be short and simple over text, email, or verbally. The only requirements are to be specific and show that you genuinely consider their points or value their contributions. Try something like, "Thank you for sending me that analysis. Points A and B were particularly interesting and helpful, and senior management will be discussing them tomorrow before we make our decision." Don't underestimate how elated and motivated your teammates will feel when their work is recognized and considered as part of a decision process. As a leader of the Pacers, Kevin Pritchard has delivered specific thank-you messages along these lines and they have made his teammates feel valued, motivated, and loyal, and given them a sense of purpose and meaning in their work.

Customized gifts are another great option, and superior to generic or often-used items, because they translate to an understanding of the individual's specific interests. The Pacers sent me a customized, framed jersey with a thank-you note after I left the organization. This type of classy gesture contributed to what will be a lifetime of goodwill, kind words, and loyalty to the organization. As noted in Chapter 2, renowned CEO Jim Sinegal of Costco proved that having loyal, appreciated ambassadors for your company creates a significant advantage.

A good way to present a special reward is by introducing it with something like, "I thought this might be a unique way to show how much I appreciate what you do around here." Imagine you work for a company in your hometown of Green Bay and have always been a rabid football fan, but surprisingly, you're not a fan of the Packers. Because your dad grew up in San Francisco, you're a lifelong 49ers fan. If your boss learned this by engaging in nonwork-related conversations with you and gave you a signed, framed Joe Montana jersey around your fifth work anniversary, how would you feel? Would that make you feel motivated, valued, and loyal? Would it increase your happiness by just a bit?

DEMEANOR

Showing caring, empathy, and various forms of recognition can be more challenging if you have a more aggressive communication style. Ask yourself if it is really working for you. Is that approach maximizing your team's performance? If not, are you open to stepping out of your comfort zone with a different approach to achieve better results?

A University of Michigan study concluded that organizations achieve better financial performance and effectiveness when leaders engage in positive practices.[26] Let's dissect this theory by analyzing two approaches with a team member who has made a mistake or struggled with their work.

The first method for you, as the leader of this individual, is to approach that person with a negative and curt tone, while taking most of their responsibility away from them. This interaction will distract your team member and make a turnaround more difficult because their mind will constantly be racing about getting fired and wondering if you'll ever trust and have confidence in them again. A vicious snowball effect will take place and their performance will likely get worse over time as their confidence declines. Consequently, if you continue this demeanor with other team members, your turnover will become high and performance outcomes will suffer. You will be stuck in a never-ending cycle of hiring with a culture that has just about no loyalty in it.

Another idea would be for you to approach this person with a positive and encouraging tone. "You've nailed this sort of thing before and grown from it. Now is your chance to do it again. I know you can handle it, and I want you to keep taking high-percentage shots with conviction. I believe in you."

Let's say you're the head coach of a basketball team. You have an elite shooter who nailed 88 percent from the free-throw line during the season. In a crucial playoff game, he is just three out of eight from the line at halftime. Do you chew him out in the locker room for lacking focus? Or do you pull him aside and tell him to brush off that first half from the line because you know he is a knock-down, lights-out shooter?

Fast-forward to the final seconds of the fourth quarter. Your team is down by one point when the player who went three for eight from the free-throw line drives to the basket and gets fouled with one second left on the clock. He has two free throws to attempt with the game on the line. Which approach you took in the locker room do you think will give the player the most confidence at making the free throws and winning the game?

Undoubtedly, the second approach will give that player better odds of coming through in the clutch. Have you had previous bosses who have taken both approaches? How did each affect your confidence and performance? Remember how each of them worked for you and choose accordingly when communicating with your team members.

This sports example is not some unrealistic new-age theory. ESPN explored this massive trend in the typically rugged National Hockey League (NHL). Building confidence through encouragement rather than criticism, particularly with younger generations, is having a powerful impact on playoff success. "The bully coach, right, wrong or different, has no chance in today's game," Detroit Red Wings coach Derek Lalonde said. "It's the reality of the players today. You still have to hold them accountable, but you have to do it in different ways."

As ESPN says, "Call it the Ted Lasso effect. The popular show is a microcosm for a shift in societal norms, which includes a new emphasis on mental health. Workplaces across multiple industries are adapting as younger generations crave different—and in many instances, less negative—environments than their predecessors. Historically, that contrasted with the high-pressure, demanding nature of professional sports. Not anymore."[27]

A big part of maintaining a positive demeanor is to stay calm when your teammates make mistakes. I learned this firsthand early on in another traditionally rough industry: the hedge fund world. A big reason why that line of business features rapid turnover is because many hedge fund managers scream at their team members and damage their mental health.

I was fortunate that my first year in the hedge fund business as an investor was strong with few hiccups. The market environment was supportive and my boss, Greg Margolis, was an excellent teacher. However, I was a naive twenty-three-year-old who thought this experience was normal. That changed in a heartbeat early in my second year.

I invested in a company called Ultimate Electronics, which proved to be a disaster. The stock was down a ton during a brutal few weeks. I was anxious about how leadership was viewing my performance and how long a leash they'd give me before firing me. These mental distractions compounded the problem, making it harder for me to focus on finding compelling new investment ideas to turn things around. I'll never forget the moment I saw Dmitry Balyasny, the head of our firm, walk toward my office. I was terrified of what he might say. He walked in, and with a quiet, matter-of-fact tone, said, "I like your approach. You have some adjustments to make to your process, but if you execute, you'll turn it around." I was stunned by his incredible calmness.

His vote of confidence in that moment provided me with the reassurance and guidance I needed to execute, which led to my discovery and evaluation of a new investment opportunity. Dmitry and the investment committee supersized that investment in the main fund. He made a bet on me while I was questioning my ability the most. This gave me unprecedented confidence and positive momentum that snowballed in the right direction, as I found other new investment ideas that also began to work.

I experienced a considerable turnaround from the awful start to have strong returns for the year, and I doubt it would have happened if I had had a leader who used the less effective "screamer" approach. Thankfully, Dmitry had my back and he proved it, showing the impactful and positive effect of a calm leadership demeanor amidst team member mistakes. It's one of many reasons Balyasny

Asset Management is one of the few large hedge funds that have thrived for over twenty years. I learned an important lesson first-hand: people don't slack off if their boss doesn't scream at them. They work even harder for a calm leader to make them proud and repay their grace, like I so desperately wanted to with Dmitry.

Another benefit of having a calm demeanor in leadership is that when leaders don't panic, their teammates won't panic, which leads to fewer mistakes. Besides that, it also contributes to a mentally healthier culture for everyone to enjoy and reap rewards.

OFFER ENHANCED MENTAL HEALTH BENEFITS

Most of us understand that mental health is important in the workplace, at home, in schools, and everywhere else people come together. But do you realize *how* important it can be in the workplace? For one thing, it translates to substantially improved KPIs in several areas.

A Harvard University study found that a properly designed wellness program can expect to yield an ROI of $3.27 to every dollar on healthcare cost reductions. Additionally, for every dollar spent on wellness programs, the companies' absenteeism-related costs fell about $2.73.[28]

The Institute of Healthcare Consumerism showed that workplace wellness programs produce an average of $5.93 to $1 savings to cost ratio, a 28-percent decrease in sick days, a 26-percent decrease in health costs, and a 30-percent decrease in costs related to workers' compensation and disability.[29]

If these numbers aren't enough to convince you of the necessity to prioritize mental health benefits in your company's culture, perhaps a personal anecdote will help.

When I transitioned from volunteer work back into a professional role for an NBA team, I chose to go with the Indiana Pacers because my diligence checks on their leadership and culture came back overwhelmingly positive. The Pacers' owner, Herb Simon, was clearly a man of high integrity who would always do the right thing. While all the feedback on the Pacers was positive, I still underappreciated how transformational of an impact their culture would have.

The Pacers' leadership provided a tremendous amount of mental health support, directly and indirectly, which was particularly noteworthy and valuable during the pandemic. That was a key reason I never wanted to leave the Pacers for another NBA team, and their turnover is so low.

My experience with a world-class organization like the Pacers has influenced many of the ideas I've used to encourage leaders to implement mental health programs in their cultures.

First, I encourage you to model the value of prioritizing mental health. If you're seeing a therapist or an executive coach, talk openly about it. The celebrity role models mentioned earlier have normalized mental health issues by speaking out about them, helping millions feel less alone. Some of your teammates may see you as a role model and find it helpful to know they're not the only one seeking out these professionals.

By sharing your experience, you'll remove any stigma associated with people who mistakenly view getting help as a weakness. By telling team members that you're seeing a professional, you can flip that mentality and have people view therapy or coaching as a proactive strength.

You could also hire a chief wellness officer whose entire job description is written around maintaining a happy, healthy, motivated culture. By dedicating a job to ensuring mental health, you are clearly sending a positive message to all of your team members about how seriously you consider the issue.

Offering healthcare plans that cover weekly visits to mental health professionals is a highly-sought benefit in today's high-stress society. Most people are willing to try a few sessions with different therapists to see if they find the right fit for them. Usually, they find someone who is helpful and come around to the idea of regular sessions. But then they come to the demoralizing realization that the visits will be over $200 apiece, so they stop going.

Money shouldn't be an obstacle to mental health, but it sadly is in many people's economic situations. There may be no greater way to show your support for these people than by footing the bill for them if your business can absorb that level of investment.

Even covering regular visits to mental health professionals may not provide people with the help they need, because many of these individuals are fully booked. It can be tough to find someone who is the right fit and has an opening in their schedule. Additionally, it can be difficult to search for professionals who are in-network or determine which nonlocal professionals offer video chat. These layers of friction make it more challenging for people who need help to follow through and get it.

If you have a chief wellness officer, they can conduct training to show team members how to easily search for in-network mental health professionals who offer video chat. Another option is to partner with companies whose purpose is to quickly connect employees to virtual therapy providers across the world, which in some cases can also be more economical.

Investing in executive coaches can have tremendous positive effects on your leaders. Scores of studies have shown that coaching pays significant ROI, with improved job satisfaction as one of the top positive outcomes.[30]

C-level executives should find an executive coach who specializes in the specific issues that their level within the organization faces. However, there are plenty of online platforms that are helpful for finding coaches for non-C-suite leaders.

Flexibility in the workplace is key for team members at all levels of the organization. A recent study by McKinsey showed flexible work as a top three motivator. If offered, 87 percent of respondents said they would use it.[31] Furthermore, a Randstad survey showed that 54 percent of white-collar workers consider job flexibility as important or more important than pay.[32] It's a new working world. Younger generations especially want and appreciate the ability to work at least partially from home, have adjusted hours (for childcare needs, etc.), and take the occasional mental health day. You must recognize the value of providing this option as a way to obtain the "A" players you need to perform for your company.

The Pacers dedicated one day every week to be free of meetings of any kind, in-person or video. The lack of distractions allowed for deep, focused work and extremely productive days. They sometimes encouraged people to leave early on Fridays ahead of long weekends, which can be helpful for beating frustrating traffic en route to a weekend getaway that recharges your well-being.

During my first two years out of college at Goldman Sachs, I was working around seventy-five hours a week and starting to feel some burnout. I asked my boss, an amazing guy named Matt Fassler, if I could leave early on Wednesdays to play pick-up hoops. As long as my work was getting done, he had no problem with it. The reason shouldn't be important. If someone asks to leave early one day a week and they're performing well, the bar should be high to refuse. By allowing them that flexibility, you build loyalty with a happier team member. It's a win-win.

MENTAL HEALTH PRACTICES TO ENCOURAGE AND SUPPORT

Four critical pillars to strong mental health and peak performance are mindfulness, sleep, exercise, and nutrition.

> *"There is no medication better than meditation."*
>
> —Marc Benioff, chairman and CEO of Salesforce

Mindfulness/meditation is a scientifically proven way to reduce stress, manage anxiety, and improve overall mental health. Mindfulness has been shown to improve workplace engagement, short-term memory, attention, and the ability to perform complex cognitive tasks.[33] [34] Many people might push this off as too "new age" for them, and that's fine. However, you should make it available to people who are open to it.

> *"You can't force people to be mindful at all, as it turns out... I think you can make it easier to be mindful... If it's on your calendar, and there's a room over there to sit in, and there's someone there to guide you, you're 10,000 times more likely to do it."*
>
> —Evan Williams, cofounder and former CEO of Twitter

Many apps exist today that can guide people through this life-changing practice. Point your team members in the right direction to find and download them. You can also dedicate a room to a meditation zone. Michael Karsch graciously hired yoga instructors to hold classes for anyone in the organization and many people took advantage of the option.

Mindfulness is linked closely to gratitude. Plenty of studies have shown that displaying gratitude significantly bolsters mental health.

"A happy person, a person who is fulfilled, deeply so, is one who is grateful."

—Robert Emmons, American psychologist
and professor at UC Davis

With an understanding that gratitude is a key element to strong mental health, how do we facilitate it in the workplace?

- Model gratitude with surprise compliments and a "thank you" every so often.
- Organize offsites with an agenda item for people to extend their appreciation for each other's work.
- Offer a small stipend for people to write and keep gratitude journals or letters of gratitude.
- Offer a stipend for people to buy and read books on gratitude. (One of my favorites is *The Little Book of Gratitude*, by Robert Emmons.)

People are just coming around to the ideas of mindfulness and gratitude as key elements to mental health. Sleep is another thing we've just begun to appreciate the value of. Historically, we've often been encouraged to work late into the evening without considering how much it may harm our sleep. The human brain only has the capacity to operate at peak performance for so long, however. Studies show that trouble sleeping leads to lower work performance, greater absenteeism, and higher healthcare costs.[35]

Instead of telling everyone to keep their noses to the grindstone around the clock, encourage good sleep habits by inviting an expert guest speaker to share science-based material on improving sleep. With the right amount of sleep, people will be more likely to perform at peak levels.

Some people just can't get past that post-lunch coma feeling, particularly because the afternoon slump is a normal part of our circadian rhythm. You can help overcome this by offering a nap room, where they can lie down for ten to twenty minutes for a much-needed refresh.

> *"Studies have shown that naps boost our immune system, lower our blood pressure, increase our ability to learn, and improve our memory and performance of complex tasks. What workplace wouldn't want a free way to do all that? Plus, nap rooms and nap pods are also a signal to employees that this is a workplace that prioritizes well-being instead of burnout."*
>
> —Arianna Huffington, CEO and founder of Thrive Global

You can also offer small stipends for people to buy and read books on how to get the sleep they need to live and work at their best. One of my favorites is *The Promise of Sleep* by William C. Dement, MD, Ph.D., who taught the most popular class at Stanford while I was an undergrad there.

While the power of mindfulness, gratitude, and sleep are emerging as more recent top priorities for mental health, exercise has been known to be great for everyone for a long time. A Harvard University study is one of several that shows that exercise boosts mental abilities like enhanced creativity, quicker learning, sharper memory, and improved concentration.[36]

Promote healthy habits through movement by having equipment on site. You can have a company gym or just a room with a bike, an all-purpose machine or two, and a few weights or kettlebells. This reduces the friction of having to leave the office to go to a gym. While I recommend *Outlive* by Peter Attia, the book's value goes far beyond exercise and is one of the world's best for overall health and longevity.

Good nutrition goes hand-in-hand with exercise as a healthy habit. Cut back on the processed and high-sugar offerings with healthy snacks like nuts, seeds, almond butter, protein powder, lentil soup, edamame, Greek yogurt, and berries in break rooms alongside green tea. If you have a cafeteria, ensure there are plenty of vegetables, whole grains, legumes, and healthy protein options such as fish, chicken, and turkey cooked with olive oil.

If you want to go all in with providing healthy nutritional options, have a guest speaker come in to talk about food and how to make positive lifestyle changes. One of my favorite books on this topic is *Eat, Drink, and Be Healthy* by Walter C. Willett, MD, DrPH, who chaired Harvard's nutrition department for twenty-six years.

An often-overlooked factor of being mentally healthy is having healthy relationships. When I was with the Pacers, they had a guest speaker come in to talk about parenting. You can invite speakers for empathy training, communication, relationships, gratitude, and many other subjects. A great read for all types of relationships is *Nonviolent Communication* by Marshall Rosenberg, PhD.

Offering financial counseling can be a welcome addition to any culture for many team members, as money is considered to be the top stressor in the vast majority of people's lives. The Wellness Barometer Survey by BrightPlan, a financial wellness benefits provider, found that 92 percent of employees are stressed about their finances. BrightPlan calculates that this anxiety is costing employers close to $200 billion annually in lost productivity. My favorite personal finance author is William J. Bernstein. His book *If You Can* is an excellent starting point for many people, particularly the younger generation.

YOUR GOAL

By following the strategies, tips, and recommendations throughout this chapter, you'll be equipped to improve your own mental health and create a culture that supports it for everyone in the organization.

Imagine how much you'll improve the lives of your team members if you follow through on a commitment to prioritize mental health. Not only will you increase the quality of life throughout your company, but you'll also develop loyalty among your team members.

At this point, we've established the key traits of a world-class culture and even formalized them in written bylaws. In the next chapter, you'll discover a hiring process to secure those oh-so-valuable "A" players, who will drive lower turnover and create space in your schedule for more strategic thinking and important aspects of your life outside of work.

LEAD WITHOUT BURNOUT

- ▶ Ensure all leaders below you learn Chapter 5's principles.
- ▶ Care deeply about your employees and show them empathy.
- ▶ Recognize your troops and show them great gestures of gratitude.
- ▶ Make your demeanor even more calm and positive.
- ▶ Go above and beyond traditional mental health benefits.

CHAPTER 6

HIRING

"The secret to my success is that we've gone to exceptional lengths to hire the best people in the world."

—Steve Jobs, cofounder, former
CEO, and chairman of Apple Inc.

Have you ever cheered for a sports team loaded with talent that is underachieving? Sometimes the lack of success can be attributed to coaching. You might watch your team play games where they don't seem as prepared as they should, or maybe the opponent's game plan looks superior in every way. This often begs the question, "With the abundance of great coaching candidates available, how did my team end up choosing this individual who isn't working out?"

The answer can be insufficient due diligence in the hiring process. The athletic director or the general manager may have flown out to meet the candidate and become so enamored with that person's style, personality, or reputation that they offered them the job within mere days of relieving the prior coach. This "process" doesn't leave time for enough rounds of interviews with everyone in the top brass, extensive reference checks, and to interview a full suite of candidates.

Such an impulsive approach can be driven by an irrational fear of missing out (FOMO) and rarely results in success. This isn't limited to sports, as insufficient hiring diligence also happens in the business world. You can't secure the "A" players who fit with your culture this way, and all the goals we've talked about so far—balance, cultural bylaws, trust, candor, and mental health—are predicated on conducting deep due diligence to land the right people you can trust.

Attracting and retaining top talent has been more difficult than ever in recent years. While the next economic downturn should increase the supply of available workers, challenges landing "A" players will likely persist to some extent due to secular trends in demographics, onshoring, and generational priorities. Retention and turnover remain a top concern among 83 percent of executives worldwide. Even more (86 percent) are concerned about a potential shortage of qualified workers in the next decade.[37]

On top of this, lesser-qualified candidates can be difficult to identify and weed out. Sadly, people may misrepresent themselves as a way of competing for the most desirable jobs. Accu-Screen, ADP, and the Society of Human Resource Managers report that 78 percent of resumes are misleading and 53 percent of them contain falsifications.

To overcome all of these challenges, you must conduct massive due diligence to build a powerhouse of talent, and we'll discuss how over the course of this chapter. Think about some of the most successful companies in the world. Microsoft's hiring process requires four to five rounds of interviews and takes anywhere from a few weeks to a few months to select the right candidate for the job. Google has a two-to-six-month process with anywhere from four to seven rounds of interviews. Make these companies serve as role models for your hiring process, as their level of due diligence has a proven track record of landing the "A" players you want.

"The cost of hiring someone bad is so much greater than missing out on someone good."

— Joe Kraus, founder of Excite,
JotSpot, and DigitalConsumer.org

STACK THE DECK

Let's get back to the sports analogy for a moment. Did you ever look at a team and think you had too much talent? Occasionally, you'll look at a team and wonder how they'll find sufficient playing time for everybody. Yet, it always seems to work itself out.

Injuries, trades, poor performance, and other variables create urgent holes to fill and lead to bench players getting more playing time. This happens in business too. There may not be as many injuries in a corporate environment as there are on a football field, but people often need to take a leave of absence to tend to their (or a loved one's) health. The best of the best will outperform their role and may take a promotion elsewhere. Others will—for one reason or another—surprise you by abruptly leaving the company. Having the talent to fill these sudden gaps in your team means you won't have to rush a bad hire.

Also, someone could be a strong performer, but increasingly too toxic to the culture to stay. Would you feel more confident moving on from them sooner if you had a deep bench of "A" players? Or, you might acquire another company and want members of your team to offload some of their existing work so they can help implement your culture and integrate the businesses.

The overall point is, you always want to be building a deep bench of "A" players even if it seems like your team is already loaded. This level of talent isn't always freely available in the marketplace and may not be around when you most urgently need them. A relevant analogy is the old adage "Raise money when you can, not when you need it." For any of the reasons stated, you'll be relieved to know that you're handing responsibilities over to another top-caliber team member.

In an ideal world, you would have "A" players from the C-Suite to the mailroom and all points in between. Is that likely to happen? Not exactly. With that understanding, on which positions should you consider focusing your greatest efforts?

Of course, you must examine what the most vital roles are for driving the most value to you given the nuances of your company and its goals.

Hiring an elite chief human resources officer (CHRO) is often a good place to start, as that person can be a powerful resource in mining top talent. They can serve as your number-one weapon in executing most of the processes for making crucial hires that fit with your culture. As team members continue to rightfully request more from the cultural element of the companies they work for, the CHRO is becoming an increasingly crucial role to any organization.

> *"If you think your CFO is more important than your CHRO, you're nuts!"*
>
> **—Jack Welch, former chairman and CEO of General Electric (GE)**

While the CHRO can help you to build, establish, and maintain the ideal culture and talent base, a chief of staff (COS) can be critical in allowing you to focus on what matters most to your professional and personal life.

By outsourcing disliked or stressful tasks that aren't in your wheelhouse to a COS, you more easily identify the parts of your job that you love and thrive at, and can increase the time you dedicate to them. The effect can be a massive improvement in well-being, your ability to stay on the job, and your impact on long-term profitability.

The COS can also help to prioritize your time and ensure the meetings you take and attend are the most crucial. Part of their job description should be to also ensure that meetings are run with ruthless efficiency. They can prioritize topics and key team member ideas for the agenda, and make sure the content is organized, synthesized, and distributed in advance so you and all attendees can optimize time. Once these are fleshed out during the meeting, they can assign appropriate action steps, as well as ensure accountability.

If you don't have an executive coach doing this for you, the COS can also choose the most impactful materials from the overwhelming amount of articles, books, podcasts, and more to assist you in strategic thinking. It can be time-consuming to identify the most relevant material from quality external sources. This is just another way the COS can become an incredibly valuable teammate.

Another prime-time player is an elite executive assistant (EA). Don't underestimate the tremendous value of having a superstar in this role. This person can be a powerhouse for productivity, scheduling, and well-being. Have them handle your professional and personal logistics, email, and calendar optimization. They can also help automate systems and institutionalize knowledge by taking notes on important topics and storing them in the cloud for future reference. This also means you only invest a lot of time in training your first EA because, if they leave, all processes are detailed in this standard operating procedure document so the next EA can hit the ground running. Lean heavily on this person to take all the administrative tasks off your plate and keep track of all back-and-forth scheduling needs with other executives and team members.

An elite EA can perform wonders in helping you to enjoy a massively improved and more organized quality of life and work. One of my CEO clients once gave me a huge hug for repeatedly encouraging him to hire an elite EA, saying, "She has been one of my most impactful hires of all time and made my life dramatically better."

TRAITS TO PRIORITIZE

Before you even write your job description, which we'll cover shortly, you need to know exactly what traits you're seeking in your candidates. After two decades of experience and researching a variety of studies, I've developed a list of top principles, talents, and skills to consider prioritizing when recruiting, hiring, and maintaining a team of "A" players.

Ensuring that candidates don't violate your cultural bylaws should be considered table stakes. Be cautious about bending this rule, as it helps to prevent any culture killers from infiltrating your organization. Professional recruitment company Robert Walters performed a study that showed 84 percent of hiring managers believe new hires perform better at their jobs when they are a good cultural fit. Strong integrity and ethics should be a requirement for any culture, as you always want people who strive—not necessarily to do what's best for themselves, but to do what's right for the team and its constituents.

Use third-party providers to test your top-performing team members for values, personality traits, and competencies. Use this profile of your "A" player characteristics to find and evaluate potential ideal candidates. If this profile doesn't match the characteristics you thought you wanted, you may need to adjust what you seek and your cultural bylaws. There are some traits in particular that every company should consider looking for in the interview process.

Seek people who are intrinsically self-motivated to learn and grow quickly. That trait indicates an infinite curiosity to be resourceful in conducting thorough research for the projects on which they work.

This goes hand in hand with open-mindedness and adaptability. You want people who don't get locked into their own opinion and closed off to input from others with different perspectives. These folks will likely show the grit it takes to persevere through roadblocks in pursuit of intellectually honest solutions. A great sign of this set of traits on a resume is when someone shows how they proactively worked to grow their skills needed for a role by acquiring a relevant certificate, degree, or other professional accreditation.

Of course, sound critical thinking, problem-solving, and decision-making processes are also vital skills to prioritize. These are particularly valuable given that artificial intelligence and other technologies have a hard time delivering on those qualities. When interviewing candidates, you can identify these traits by finding out what a candidate would do in a typical problem situation at your company. Ask about their process, reasoning, and everything that factors into the ultimate decision they would make.

Additional top-flight qualities to seek in your candidate include organization and high attention to detail. When people organize their work with precision, information is always readily available for you or coworkers when they need it. When you know they get all the little details correct, you feel confident enough in their reliability and execution that you don't think twice when delegating somewhat higher-profile responsibilities to them. They are more likely to follow through and deliver.

ENHANCED JOB DESCRIPTIONS

Whether you're formally posting a job opening or relying on other methods, always create a job description that attracts the right candidates for each role. Don't go through the motions by creating a templated job description for every new hire. Remember, you're talking to someone who is not only highly skilled but has many choices about where to take those skills. Ideally, you want to sell top talent on why your company is right for them and differentiated from other possible companies.

State your company's purpose for existence and what you're trying to do with it in the marketplace. Tell them about some of your cultural bylaws and how they are different from other companies. Your goal is to connect with a certain type of candidate—one who would love your culture and aspirations—on an emotional level. Inspire them to see you as a better fit with their values and goals than another company into which they may be looking.

Instead of a basic job summary, use descriptive language to paint a vivid picture of the overarching purpose of the specific role you're looking to fill. How does that role relate to the cultural bylaws and goals you just laid out? This will add purpose, meaning, and a connection to something bigger than themselves for even the lowest-level roles. For example, if you're looking for a custodial professional for a sports arena, tell the story of how critical it is to take pride in keeping the arena clean to help the company continue to maximize the fan experience. You can even talk about how cherished memories are created by parents taking their children to games. Every part of their experience inside the stadium can play a crucial role in that tradition and inspire those families to return for more memories.

Instead of simply listing broad job responsibilities, detail the specific tasks they'll do and highlight the outcomes you're hoping to achieve from that work. This is an additional step to ensure each person reading the job description understands that even the task-oriented grunt work has meaning and a reason behind it. A somewhat disturbingly high 61 percent of new hires have said there are aspects of the job that are different from the expectations that were set in the hiring process.[38] This speaks to an even more eye-opening realization, which is that 91 percent of team members consider quitting a job within the first month if the job doesn't match their expectations.[39] Think of how much time and money is wasted in the interview process if you lose an "A" player right away due to unclear expectations.

Upgrade the typical "qualifications" section. Detail the skills needed to execute the outcomes you highlighted earlier. Also, lay out the specific traits you're seeking to fit your cultural bylaws. The same Robert Walters study mentioned previously found that 73 percent of team members leave because of a misaligned cultural fit.

Borrow a great technique from *Topgrading* by Bradford Smart. Make it clear in the job description that you'll ask each candidate to arrange for several reference calls with former bosses and others. The best candidates have nothing to hide and will be happy that you're taking the time to call people who know them and their work ethic. Those with something to hide will likely shy away from applying, saving you from wasting time reading their resume and interviewing them.

Finish job descriptions with ratings and testimonials from customers and team members. This social proof of experience has been a big advantage for companies in winning customers; it can be equally effective when competing for talent.

CONSIDERING THE CANDIDATES

After you've created a job application that compels "A" players to apply, you need to go through the list of applicants and begin the process of finding the right person for the role.

Resist the temptation to narrow your list of potential winners too much in the beginning. You want a large initial sample size to choose from because you don't want to hastily throw away an underappreciated fit. The best of the best sometimes don't look great on paper. They may only emerge in the interview process.

Some of your applicants will be referrals from current team members, colleagues, and other sources close to your inner circle. These people are often your best choices to advance to the interview stage for the following reasons:

1. Your trusted source is putting their reputation on the line in referring this candidate. This lowers the odds you're wasting time interviewing them.
2. A Glassdoor study showed referred candidates are more likely to say yes to an offer.[40] This is likely because they trust the person who referred them, and that person has already sold them on your culture.
3. Referrals cost substantially less than recruiting external candidates.

As William Arruda of *Forbes* pointed out, new benchmarking data from the Society for Human Resource Management states that many employers estimate the total cost to hire a new team member can be three to four times the position's salary.[41] You can make a serious dent in costs related to your hiring process by using referrals. In fact, 55 percent of company representatives have reported savings from referral programs.[42] Additionally, a JobVite Index study showed referral candidates get hired 55 percent faster than those hired through a career site, proving added savings in you and your company's most precious resource—time.

Ask applicants to complete a sample assignment. When I attended Stanford, the administrators allowed us to audit classes before committing to them. I (and other students) found this to be helpful because it provided experience and insight I couldn't get anywhere else. Your job candidates will feel the same way and you'll garner a lot of information about them as well.

Choose an assignment typical to the tasks they would be tackling or problems they would be solving, so you can learn if they fit your desired qualifications. Give specific instructions to include or address certain things so you can test their attention to detail. The candidate's response should allow you to eliminate people based on low quality, errors, or insufficient relevant skills. Additionally, many people will drop out when they realize the role isn't well-suited to their current desires or skills. When you drop someone off the list or they do it themselves, that's a fantastic result because it saves time.

MASSIVE DUE DILIGENCE IN INTERVIEWS

Executing multiple rounds of interviews with different people is key because crowds have greater wisdom at forecasting than an individual. By having several people evaluate candidates, you eliminate the risk of an individual's bias against someone, or a person winning due to irrelevant common ground. You don't want someone to get eliminated because they had an off day, but you also don't want someone to get hired because they shared a love for Nebraska football with the person who interviewed them.

Ensure every interviewer knows in advance that they'll have to rate the candidates on each of the key things you're seeking. Examples of "rating categories" include cultural fit, each of the top three traits needed for that job, and other key characteristics to have (such as intrinsic motivation, critical thinking, and attention to detail). Your CHRO can take the weight you assign to each category and calculate the total score for each candidate. Of course, this won't be the sole determinant in who you hire. However, it is a scientific process for quantifying each candidate's strengths and weaknesses, and it limits the emotional biases and flaws of traditional hiring decision discussions.

Ratings are submitted before everyone gets together to discuss candidates. That way, you limit groupthink, the most vocal champion in the room winning out, or people watering down the negatives of candidates initially referred by others in the room.

Before digging into questions, I like to start by repeating the *Top-grading* technique from the job description. "I'll be asking candidates who advance to future rounds to arrange for several reference calls with former bosses and others. Is that OK with you?" Pay attention to body language and see who gets uncomfortable.

Your company likely has specific needs and questions to ask. However, my list of effective interview questions may provide inspiration for the answers you need to recognize "A" players in the interview process. A few were inspired by some of the most influential people I've followed in my career. These include Bradford Smart and his book *TopGrading*; Geoff Smart and his book *Who*; Tyler Cowen and Daniel Gross with their book, *Talent*; and world-class guests from the Tim Ferriss podcast.

Q. **"What are you really good at? Provide examples of how you've used those strengths in the past to add value to businesses with goals and challenges like ours."**

The purpose of this question is to find out if the candidate has truly studied your business, goals, challenges, and job description. If so, they will intentionally highlight a strength to something related. Can you see how they used those strengths before as being applicable to your specific issues or goals?

Q. **"What is your experience with X, Y, and Z tasks? Tell me about the outcomes you've achieved."**

Be a little more direct with this question because you want to know if they have specific experience with tasks related to the role for which they're applying. Their answer will help to determine whether in previous roles they were actively involved and creating beneficial outcomes for the company or just showing up to get a paycheck.

Q. "What are the biggest mistakes you think our company is currently making? How would you approach these situations differently?"

This question can be a differentiator. If the candidate isn't good at critical thinking, they'll likely stumble on this one. If they've studied your company in-depth, this is their opportunity to showcase what they've learned and the ideas they bring to the table. Do they have the confidence to speak up and challenge you? This question will uncover the meek, the unprepared, and the uninspired.

Q. "What do you read in your spare time to sharpen your knowledge?"

The answer to this question should be instinctive. Most knowledge seekers are ready to talk about the podcasts, blogs, books, etc. they find most interesting and helpful. You're hoping to hear something that signals the person is intellectually curious, has a growth mindset, and is looking for ways to become more well-rounded.

Q. "What is your process for staying on top of things?"

Everyone is busy. With 1,001 things going on in everybody's life, you want to find out how the candidate deals with it all. Are they organized? Do they have a good system to ensure they get the right things done on time? What does their attention to detail look like? You want to find answers to these questions within their answer to the larger question. The candidate's response here should say a lot about how reliable they are in following through, or whether things will get lost in the shuffle.

Q. "What would your last few bosses say about your strengths and weaknesses? How would they rate you overall on a scale of one to ten?"

This is an especially good indicator of how self-aware and honest the candidate is. Are they in denial about their weaknesses? Or do they have a level of humility and candor that will be appreciated by their team members? You'll find out for certain when you chat with their old bosses!

Q. "What about our culture makes you want to work with us?"

If the candidate is specifically interested in your company's culture, they'll prove it here by responding quickly with elements of your culture they've researched. If they show an authentic passion for why they want to join your company, they're more likely to say yes to an offer, work well within the culture, and stay in the job.

Q. "Which of our values are least aligned with your own?"

The person you're interviewing might be ready for the previous question, but they might not have given this one much thought. You're looking for how much they know about your company's values and whether there are any potential deal-breakers here. You want validation that they know what your company stands for and that they'll embrace the culture that promotes it.

Q. "What other companies do you affiliate with (for example, purchase their products) because you believe in what they stand for?"

You'll learn how much they truly pay attention to company values as opposed to simply studying yours for this interview so they could say what you want to hear.

Q. "What motivates you to work?"

Intrinsic motivation is a key character trait of top talent. Learn more about what makes them tick.

Q. "What are the most counter-consensus views you hold and why do you think you're right? Which counterarguments have altered your thinking and lowered your conviction? What would it take for you to completely change your view?"

You're testing for whether they'll bring contrarian ideas to the table and how susceptible the person is to groupthink. You'll also learn how open-minded they are to learning and adapting from high-candor debate. The sweet spot is someone who is contrarian enough to present outside-the-box options, but open-minded enough to listen, value, and incorporate the opinions of others.

Q. "Tell me about a tough situation you were in or a mistake you made. How did you come to your decision, and what lessons did you learn from the outcome?"

"A" players should be able to admit mistakes and learn from the experience. The candidate's answer to this question will shed a lot of light on their humility, their capacity for growth, and their thought process in making tough decisions.

Q. "If you join our team and it doesn't work out, what is the most likely reason why?"

You might learn about a weakness that is a dealbreaker with this question. Evaluate the response for any potential conflicts with the role.

Q. "What percentage of the time do you follow through on what you say you're going to do? What are the most common reasons you're not able to follow through?"

This is a good question to give you insight into their reliability and limitations.

Q. "What questions do you have for me?"

Always finish with this. It is one of the most important questions of all of them. Every candidate should have at least five questions for you to answer. Anything less indicates a lack of effort, research, or genuine care for the position. This is a dead red indicator of how resourceful they'll be on the job. It also indicates whether they have several options and are evaluating you, which should be true of most "A" players, or are desperate and willing to take anything.

When I was twenty-three and interviewed for the job at Balyasny, the firm's chief investment officer, Dmitry Balyasny, asked me this question. I kept going on and on with questions. Eventually, Dmitry said, "Hey, I have to get to the airport for a flight to Chicago." So I said I would walk him to his car and kept asking questions in the elevator. He followed up with, "If you're as diligent with researching investments as you are with asking about our company, you'll be a good analyst." I suspect Dmitry offered the job to me partly because of what he learned from asking that critical interview question.

Massive due diligence in the interview process could take weeks to months to find the best candidates for each role, but it's worth the time investment. Think about how long it takes to make a major decision such as an M&A, marketing strategy, or pursuing a product line. Would it make sense not to take the same time and level of diligence in determining the right people to be involved in the decision-making of those critical items?

If you're a senior executive of a medium-large-sized business, you don't need to be involved in the early stages of the interview process. Let your elite CHRO and other trustworthy team members narrow the field so you're only spending your valuable time with the small group of top remaining candidates.

CHECKING WITH REFERENCES

After the interview process, you should have a list of candidates whittled down to the top three or so potential winners. At that point, it's time to call their references. A good idea is to call the ones they've chosen, as well as other former bosses and colleagues whom they didn't list and prep to say only nice things.

When calling references, assure the person you speak to that they have 100 percent confidentiality: Nothing will ever be traceable back to them and this call is just one of dozens of reasons the candidate may or may not get the job. Both of these comments should make them more open. People don't want their honest feedback to be the primary reason someone didn't get a job.

Here are some of my favorite questions to ask during reference calls:

- *"How resourceful are they with the attitude and grit to always find ways to overcome challenges?"*
- *"How reliable and organized are they to always get their work done on time and accurately?"*
- *"The number-one concern or weakness that's coming up is X. What do you think about that? Do you have a different concern or weakness from when you worked together?"*
- *"If I'm hiring a partner to balance their strengths and weaknesses, what type of person would I look for?"*

The prior two questions are framed to make them more open to discussing the candidate's weaknesses.

- *"How do you think they would fit in this specific job and culture?"*
- *"When they disagree with you or another person, how open-minded are they to learning the right answer and adapting their view?"*
- *"How would you rate the quality of their decision-making process?"*
- *"I am not passing this information back to the candidate. On a scale of one to ten, what is your level of endorsement and why?"*

The rating provides much more insight than a simple yes or no, as you will rarely hear no. If you hear a six, seven, or even eight, that's not very favorable. You want a raving fan, not a passive supporter hedging their endorsement.

- *"What advice would you give me on how to best manage the candidate for success?"*

This question helps you hit the ground running with a great start with the candidate you hire.

- *"Is there anything else important I should know about them that I haven't asked?"*

Now you've finished your reference calls and have whittled your list down to one to three finalists. Remember the third-party testing you used to identify the most common values, personality traits, and competencies of your top employees? Consider running top finalists through it as another evidence-based data point that can raise or lower your conviction in their fit.

SELL THEM ON YOU

If you've done thorough diligence and selected a true "A" player to recruit, you'll likely be in competition for them. You must be ready to give it your all when trying to win over top talent, much like you would when competing for business.

Highlight how you're different from key competitors they may be considering. Walk them through each cultural bylaw and show them you like them because they're a great fit. The Cialdini Liking Principle comes into play again here, as this makes the candidate more likely to like you. Tell them that by joining your team, they will find purpose and meaning in contributing to something bigger than themselves.

Emphasize how your culture prioritizes mental health. Flesh out the details of how your workplace promotes flexibility, balance, and two-way clear/honest feedback. Proudly state other nonmonetary perks, like childcare, hybrid or remote-friendly work, casual dress, bring-your-dog-to-work day, etc. If there are any nonsalary add-ons you gleaned that would be uniquely important to them, mention your openness in considering them. This is your opportunity to win an "A" player over a competitor.

Most of all, emphasize that you genuinely care about each team member in your organization. Make it clear that there is no ceiling to their career and you'll do whatever it takes to help them reach their goals.

CELEBRATE NEW HIRES

When you're particularly effective in the hiring process, you'll notice a steep increase in the level of top talent in your business. Anytime you land a new teammate, celebrate them! There are a few options for doing this.

You could deliver them a welcome card signed by their new colleagues. Have it waiting for them on their desk on day one. Another option is to set aside thirty minutes of an afternoon for the team to share celebration cake together (food offerings don't need to be healthy 100 percent of the time) and deliver the signed card. You could also consider giving the new person a small gift in advance of their joining the team.

One of my clients personally speaks to *every* new team member. Some of them are frontline contributors who are blown away by the CEO of a large company taking the time to sit and talk with them about the company's history, culture, and how important that person will be, as a contributor. Little things like this mean a lot to people who are truly looking to join a company for reasons beyond a paycheck.

Imagine the confidence you'll have after conducting such due diligence to bring in plenty of "A" players. Knowing that you've put so much work into bringing in the best talent available will make it easy for you to trust them and outsource more to your team. It all contributes to a greater level of work-life optimization and strategic thinking time.

No matter how much you fill your business with "A" players and delegate work to their utterly capable hands, you will still have important workloads. After all, you are a business leader. Rest assured, more can be done to help you and your team become even more efficient and productive. Find out more in the next chapter about how to make the most of your time and enjoy a more holistic lifestyle.

LEAD WITHOUT BURNOUT

▶ Build a deep bench of "A" players even if you're a bit overstaffed.

▶ An elite CHRO, COS, and EA can be game-changers for your life.

▶ Find high-integrity cultural fits who are intrinsically self-motivated, have sound critical thinking processes, and possess the key traits to execute and get results.

▶ Follow world-class processes for extensive due diligence across interviewing and reference checks.

▶ Know how to sell top talent on you and celebrate them once on board.

CHAPTER 7

OPTIMIZING TIME

"Focus on essentials and try not to get distracted and bogged down by things that don't add value to the bottom line."

—Carlos Slim, Mexican business
magnate, investor, and philanthropist

One of your biggest challenges in optimizing personal and professional growth is time. We've already mentioned how easily a business leader can get caught up in all the minutiae. Getting highly involved with problem-solving is likely one reason you've risen to the rank you now hold. You're used to putting out fires, so people know you're the one to get things done. Perhaps you haven't set the right boundaries yet. Even if you have, you may still find there just aren't enough hours in a day to fulfill all of the things for which you consider yourself responsible. It's time to change that.

By learning and using three key skills—the Pareto Principle, snapshots, and calendar analysis—you will be equipped to optimize your time. This will allow space to scale your business while creating more time to enjoy whatever you value most in life. Snapshots and calendar analysis are two of the top tools I've honed to optimize productivity, but they can't exist without a familiar friend called the 80/20 rule (aka the Pareto Principle). Chances are you've already heard of this concept, but let's dive into the specifics of how you can apply it to effectively lead without burnout.

FINDING FOCUS WITH THE 80/20 RULE

Although he didn't invent the original concept that 80 percent of outcomes come from 20 percent of the causes, Richard Koch wrote a famous book called *The 80/20 Principle*. In it, he provides several examples of how the rule can be applied in business and life.

- 80 percent of family problems are caused by 20 percent of the issues.
- 80 percent of grief is caused by 20 percent of the people in your life.
- 80 percent of crimes are committed by 20 percent of criminals.
- 80 percent of sales are from 20 percent of clients. Are your customers the number-one constituent in your bylaws, and how can you better serve the best ones?
- 80 percent of a company's output is produced by 20 percent of its workers. You can land a lot more of these 20-percent workers (or "A" players) when you execute on Chapter 5.
- 80 percent of complaints are by 20 percent of customers. Could your long-term productivity, profits, or returns on capital be better if you pruned some customers who are high maintenance or minimal contributors to the bottom line?

Those are excellent examples of how to optimize results by focusing on the highest-impact causes. With Koch's examples as inspiration, I've highlighted several examples that I have witnessed or experienced in my professional career.

- 80 percent of financial portfolio gains came from 20 percent of investments made.
- 80 percent of a team's wins can often be attributed to 20 percent of its players.

- 80 percent of my clients' stress comes from 20 percent of the issues in their lives.

Take a deep dive into your company's situation. You may discover that 80 percent of what you or your team does in a typical workday will not have a significant impact on your long-term growth prospects, profitability, and returns on capital. Why give so much attention to many things that won't move the needle? Instead, focus on the 20 percent that will have the biggest impact.

To maximize your team's output, you must communicate and reward the 20 percent of priorities that matter most. Workplace analytics company Visier Inc. showed that an alarming 43 percent of workers admit to spending more than ten hours a week trying to look productive instead of focusing their time on valuable tasks. Why do workers prioritize tasks that make them most visible to others? They believe they'll appear more valuable and it will prove critical to their professional success. Avoiding this lost productivity is a huge advantage for elite cultures of trust and candor, where top bylaws and priorities are regularly emphasized and rewarded.[43]

To be clear, you can't ignore all of that less-meaningful 80 percent. Some of these are administrative tasks that must get done to conduct your business. In other cases, executing some of the little details with great care helps the top 20 percent bear fruit. But imagine the impact of devoting nearly all of your focus to the much more impactful 20 percent. The results can be astounding!

"Focus does not mean saying yes. It means saying no."

—Steve Jobs, cofounder, former
CEO, and chairman of Apple Inc.

IDENTIFY YOUR BIG THREE

From my time on Wall Street investing in companies, and my experience coaching CEOs, I've found that three key issues will largely determine if a company will successfully achieve its goals. Start by reducing the fifteen initiatives, twenty-five items on your to-do list, and fifty topics you'll discuss in upcoming meetings down to a top three. How?

Have your CFO or finance team quantify the potential impact of the initiatives and items up for discussion. For example, they could be potential acquisitions, expanding into new product lines, and pursuing untapped geographies. Once your finance team runs forecasts on these various items, see which are projected to have the greatest impact on EBITDA and returns on capital over the next five to ten years. This exercise can help you rank the three areas of highest strategic priority. By identifying the biggest needle-moving items, you'll achieve much better results than by applying a shotgun approach to all the items on your plate.

I used the Big Three approach on Wall St. to try to optimize the returns in my portfolio. There were plenty of ideas and leads I could have chased. Before committing to weeks of work, I had to quantify some things about each potential investment to determine which ones could make a big enough difference.

- Is the daily volume of shares traded so low that I won't be able to buy much stock without driving up the price? If so, I'd never be able to buy enough stock to have a big impact on my portfolio's returns.
- This stock may have only 8 percent upside to earnings if my thesis works out, but huge downside potential that could crush my returns if I'm wrong. That also wouldn't deserve being on the Big Three to-do list.
- Are there catalysts that could play out soon for a stock, so it deserves consideration at the top of my to-do list, or will the turnaround take a long time to play out?

My year was often determined by how well I prioritized my list of ideas for investment. If I spent too much time focusing on ideas that wouldn't provide big enough value or nonurgent matters, the opportunity cost could have been huge. If you do the same, a competitor may beat you to a lucrative new geography, product line, or acquisition.

OPTIMIZING THE EISENHOWER MATRIX

Identifying only three items to focus on might sound like a great idea, but how else do you make it happen aside from you or your finance team quantifying things? As a busy leader, you probably have over a hundred things to consider, maybe more. For the answer, let's revisit an old productivity tool that was first adapted decades ago. You're going to learn a more modernized version of the Eisenhower Matrix that I have honed.

Originally conceived by President Dwight Eisenhower and popularized by Steven Covey, the Eisenhower Matrix is a powerful framework that can help you to prioritize your most critical agenda items. I've studied it in detail and have optimized it in a way that has produced fruitful results for me and my coaching clients.

Take a blank piece of paper and draw a big plus sign in the middle, creating four quadrants. In the lower-right corner, list items that are **neither important nor urgent.** Cross those off of yours and everyone else's to-do list. If there are items there that absolutely must get done at some point for a logistical reason, hand them off to an assistant or a team member with a role that is much lower in the organizational hierarchy.

These items clearly don't fall within the 20 percent of most impactful things you can do as a leader or as a unit.

Label the space in the lower-left corner as **not important but urgent.** Give those items to an "A" player that you trust, and assign complete freedom to execute in whatever ways they think will provide the best results. Let them make the final decisions and be responsible for the outcomes without involving you. Simply remind them to think about it using the 80/20 rule. Convey to them that this item is not very important, so don't spend a lot of time on it, but execute the urgent parts that matter most.

These items also do not meet the criteria for the 20 percent on which you should be focusing.

In the upper-right corner of the matrix, you'll list items that are **important, but not urgent.** Put these items on your calendar for specific dates when they are likely to move into the urgent category. If you know of a deadline that is coming for October 8th, but it's only the first of June, place a reminder on your calendar that leaves an appropriate amount of time to get the task done by the due date. This is a tremendous method for reducing anxiety, as it gets items off your mind in the short term, and it puts you at ease because you know you have time allotted for it in the future. You're not procrastinating. Rather, you're postponing items of lesser urgency for a more appropriate time.

This quadrant does meet the criteria for the 20 percent of the business on which you should be focusing, just not right now. When it moves into the urgent category, you'll want to determine exactly how important it is. The higher the level of importance, the more of it you will execute yourself. The lower the level of importance, the more likely you can allow your "A" players to run with the first 90 percent and loop you in for the last 10 percent to approve or make the final decision.

Only one quadrant contains the 20 percent items that you must do now: it is the upper-left one, labeled **important and urgent.** This is your main area of focus as a leader—the items on which you should be focusing the majority of your attention. Make a detailed game plan for these items and take action on them immediately. Given the urgency, find "A" players that have the necessary skills and allow them to contribute and shine. This has the benefit of making them feel fulfilled while you free up time to focus on the most critical aspects within the most impactful 20 percent of your business.

OPTIMIZED EISENHOWER MATRIX

Important **Urgent**	**Important** **Not Urgent**
Focus most of your attention on these now.	Put them on the calendar for when they become urgent.
Not Important **Urgent**	**Not Important** **Not Urgent**
Outsource to an "A" player for them to decide and execute.	Cross off everyone's to-do lists, and assign must-dos to an EA.

By clarifying importance and urgency, then correctly placing those items in the optimized Eisenhower Matrix, you and your team will know exactly which three items make up the 20 percent of high-impact causes that require the bulk of your focus.

> *"The key to having more time is doing less, and there are two paths to get there, both of which should be used together: 1) define a short to-do list, and 2) define a not-to-do list."*
>
> —Tim Ferriss, American entrepreneur, investor, author, podcaster, and lifestyle guru

PUTTING THE 80/20 TAKEAWAYS INTO ACTION

The preceding information does nothing if you don't put it into action. Simply storing it in your mind will not provide any tangible results. After you've performed the analysis in the optimized Eisenhower Matrix, translate the four quadrants into a running to-do list that syncs across all devices through a tool such as Evernote or Outlook. That way, you'll always know the most critical items to attack from your to-do list, whether you're on a laptop, phone, tablet, or whatever comes next.

Having a digitally stored prioritized list on you at all times during the workday is one step in the right direction. The next is to figure out how you work best.

Most people can only work in limited chunks of time before the quality of their work degrades. A recent study by the Draugiem Group found that the most productive 10 percent of people work, on average, in fifty-two-minute chunks with seventeen-minute breaks.[44]

In the *Art of Learning,* John Waitzkin says the key to performance is a brief period of serene relaxation between times of physically and mentally pushing yourself.

Personally, I've discovered that I work best in forty-five to sixty-minute bursts, followed by fifteen-minute breaks that involve one of three things.

1. Walking outside. Research by the Mayo Clinic has linked sitting for long periods of time with numerous health concerns, like high blood pressure, high blood sugar, excess body fat around the waist, and unhealthy cholesterol levels.[45] Also, the *Journal of the American Medical Association* (JAMA) has shown physical and psychological benefits from walking ten thousand steps per day and being out in fresh air with trees.[46] Furthermore, a study published at the Yale School of Environment claims a growing number of studies point to significant benefits from being in nature.[47] Walking outside is

particularly impactful during 2:00-3:00 p.m., when circadian rhythms and energy levels become lower.

2. Engaging in something personally fun or interesting. I enjoy reading articles, self-improvement books, and checking the box scores of my favorite sports teams. I also "geek out" with economic data and charts impacting the outlook and investment landscape. You might enjoy different activities. Whatever they are, make time for them.

3. Completing small, easy work tasks that don't require much mental energy. You might also find these breaks to be a good opportunity to read short-form leadership articles that were published since your last time dedicated to strategic thinking.

These examples are excellent uses of your productivity-enhancing break time, but you can come up with your own as well. With all the podcasts, websites, and other forms of media available, the options are nearly limitless. Don't forget to get outside as well, given the proven benefits of being in nature. Plenty of hiking trails, parks, and beaches exist all over the world. Surely, several of them are close by for you to enjoy and decompress.

THE SURPRISING, UNDENIABLE POWER OF SNAPSHOTS

In a modern society where something demands your attention for just about every minute of every hour in every day, it can be next to impossible to remember the most critical learnings and put them to good use. So you might try other tricks to jog your memory.

One of the most popular, but severely deficient, methods you might use to remember key pieces of information is the big yellow highlighter when reading a book. As you read, you highlight what you perceive as the most relevant information to remember. Read, highlight, rinse, repeat for the next three hundred pages or so. How often do you go back and reread the highlighted passages? Almost never.

Another approach to mentally refresh is scribbling within the margins of various papers, a notepad, or sticky notes on your desk. The result? Usually countless sheets of loose paper littering your desk with no discernable method of finding what you need when you need it.

The *Wall Street Journal* has reported that most people lose an average of one hour per day searching for misplaced information. Tomorrow, you will likely waste one hour of your life looking for things you highlighted, jotted down, or tried to store in your memory. The same thing will happen the next day and the day after that. You will have spent too much of your precious time as an explorer of misplaced or forgotten information, rather than a business leader. That is a huge opportunity cost. Think of the value of the strategic thinking you could have done in that time. If you want to get that time back, use one of my favorite productivity-enhancing ideas: I call them snapshots.

Create individual documents in Microsoft Word, Google Docs, or whatever software with which you're most comfortable. These will be separate summaries of each important topic in your business, much like CliffsNotes for popular books. Always remember to save these items to the cloud for reference later. Also, encourage your team members to use snapshots. Productivity can go up exponentially when everybody is able to locate information on demand.

The key to making snapshots work is to remember not to put everything in them. Being too detailed defeats the purpose. Use the 80/20 rule when creating them. Only include the 20 percent that's the most relevant information.

MY CRITICAL TOOL AS AN INVESTOR

I started using snapshots as a hedge fund investor. When I began evaluating consumer stocks, I employed a nineteen-step research process. It provided a ton of information, but it was impossible to remember. As a result, much of it would get lost. It would have been fine if I only lost the least important facts, but I lost an equal percentage of critical knowledge.

My resolution was to start by developing one foundational document in Microsoft Word. I called it the Consumer Stocks Snapshot. This included the most critical categories and items I needed to know about each consumer company I researched to determine if the stock was likely to go up or down. As I researched each company, I would fill in answers as to how they stacked up on these critical categories and items. I would save this customized snapshot of the 20 percent of my most valuable research for each company. I would name them "Best Buy Snapshot," "Home Depot Snapshot," etc. This gave me an easily accessible source to tap whenever a decision needed to be made about a stock, sometimes under immense time pressure.

As a hedge fund investor, snapshots proved to be a critical tool. Since they were stored in one place in the cloud, not only was I able to access information quickly, but I never forgot anything crucial again. Snapshots also made it incredibly easy to compare two alternative stocks as apples to apples, since I had similar categories of information on both. Think about the possibilities for using the same approach as a business leader. If you're considering several acquisitions, you could gather the most critical categories for consideration, create a snapshot of each possible transaction and compare them side by side in a more systematic way.

When I started at Karsch Capital, nearly fifty brokers from sell-side research firms reached out to ask how they could be of service to me; one in particular stood out. Her name was Lisa, and she worked for a boutique firm that did not have a reputation like the big players—J.P. Morgan, Goldman Sachs, etc. She was up against giants of industry and it was going to be an uphill battle for her to stand out. But she did it.

I explained all of my preferences for receiving information to the brokers. For example, I told them that I didn't want a morning voicemail saying that my analyst upgraded stocks X, Y, and Z. That voicemail wasn't helpful to me and I would delete it without listening to it. Before I even walked in the door in the morning, I would have read about that in my email, so I didn't want to waste any precious time with repetitive information. Instead, I only wanted them to call me after an analyst spoke with a management team and learned something interesting.

Of all the brokers, Lisa stood out the most at providing me with all the information I wanted and none of what I didn't. Why? Because she took detailed notes when I gave my preferences for information. She used her own version of a snapshot, keying in my requests for information in a quickly accessible format that she could reference repeatedly. As a result, she executed with consistent precision and quality of information. Lisa became one of my most trusted brokers.

PRESENTATION PREPARATION

For roughly twenty years, I've been conducting research and taking electronic notes on how to give impactful speeches. I have a "Speaking Snapshot" stored in the cloud for how to execute the most important parts of an effective speech, from stories to interactive content.

After moving from New York to Sacramento, I decided to take a few years off from public speaking. When I was hired by a hedge fund to present again, I was able to pick right back up where I left off, like no time had passed, simply by referring back to my

Speaking Snapshot. You can enjoy the same benefit when you re-visit potential acquisitions, initiatives, or hires you may have passed on several years ago.

COACHING NOTES

Today, I use snapshots for common situations that arise with my executive coaching clients. For example, a client might ask me about the most revealing questions to ask when checking refer-ences for a potential new CFO. In some cases, the wording matters a lot, so I want to give them the questions verbatim.

Fortunately, business isn't like a high school algebra test; you can use reference notes. So, I search for the correct section of the snap-shot on my laptop. Then I can give them the exact scripts for ques-tions they should ask.

My client may then transition to seeking my counsel on a major personal issue. The first thing I want to do in that situation is help lessen the acute anxiety around it. Fortunately, there are scores of evidence-based techniques for reducing anxiety. They often involve specific questions to answer, and I can't know definitively which ones will work best for each person. Since it's impossible to mem-orize all of them, it's beneficial to have a snapshot that is easily accessible.

SIMPLIFYING THE HIRING PROCESS

One of the most beneficial ways to use snapshots as a business leader is in the hiring process. You and your CHRO can work to-gether to create one foundational "Hiring Snapshot" with the crit-ical categories you're seeking in candidates. Then customize one for each candidate whom you're seriously considering adding to your team. Gather their strengths and weaknesses in each of these cate-gories you find to be the most crucial, save them to the cloud, and conduct a side-by-side comparison. Both may have great potential, but one might jump out at you as the next "A" player to onboard when you use this apples-to-apples comparison process.

By having snapshots of highly qualified candidates stored in the cloud, you also have a "standby" list of people, who didn't make it to your team but could be considered for future hires.

EMPLOYEE ENGAGEMENT

Beyond the hiring process, you can use snapshots for each key team member as a talent retention tool. Keep a list of their long-term goals, their specific feedback on you as a leader, and how you can support them. Store this information so that you can regularly check in on how you're executing on their development. By including a list of things the team member enjoys most, you can also refer to these to express gratitude. Suppose an employee knocked a project out of the park and you want to show your appreciation. If you check their snapshot and it reminds you they're a wine enthusiast who loves a specific type of California cab, you can send them one from their favorite winery. Similarly, if you spot a team member struggling and in need of a pick-me-up, you can send them a customized gift with a message that reminds them of your faith in their abilities.

CLIENT RELATIONSHIP ENHANCER

If you're the leader of a client-facing business like Lisa was, use snapshots for referencing personal and professional information on the clients. If the person has two kids named Mia and James, put it in the snapshot. Include your clients' hobbies, favorite sports teams, beloved charities, preferences for receiving information, and anything else you can think of that will help you to establish a close connection. Having all this information available makes it easier to execute more customized emails, phone calls, and thoughtful gifts. A good example of something similar can be found in the food service industry. Well-run restaurants keep profiles on their diners' preferences, food allergies, and other information to maximize their experience.

The following is a highly simplified mini snapshot—a few sample categories—that you might use in a client-facing business. You would answer the bolded/underlined categories for each client and save their individual snapshots separately.

CLIENT SNAPSHOT: ROBERT SMITH

BUSINESS

- **His most important business goal:** To provide his own customers with a wide selection of products as well as speedy service
- **Friction/roadblocks he is experiencing with our service:** His teams are often slowed down by the processes in our ordering systems; we don't provide enough variety in XYZ product lines
- **How I can help him achieve his goals and have a better experience with us:** Work with internal teams to reduce steps/friction in the ordering process, work with product development to see where testing product line expansion makes sense

PERSONAL

- **Family:** Twelve-year-old son James, eight-year-old daughter Mia, wife named Jennifer
- **Hobbies:** Golf, skiing, reading true crime novels
- **Alma Maters:** Undergraduate degree from Harvard, MBA from Wharton
- **Favorite teams:** Mets, Giants, Knicks, Rangers
- **Favorite charities:** Against Malaria Foundation, Make-A-Wish Foundation, Special Olympics

JOB NOTES

Standard operating procedures (SOPs) are another great fit for snapshots. Each job in the company may require a different set of practices. Have the team leader in each department input them into a snapshot. This will involve time investment upfront, but productivity will skyrocket in the long term. When a team member leaves and a new hire steps in, having the SOPs ready will reduce knowledge loss and training time. They will help them get acquainted with their job much more quickly.

RUTHLESS PRIORITIZATION OF YOUR CALENDAR

"It's not the daily increase but daily decrease. Hack away at the unessential."

—Bruce Lee, Hong Kong and American martial artist

Mastering the 80/20 rule and snapshots are two time-optimization techniques that can transform your leadership efficiency. The third is calendar analysis.

Management consulting firm Russell Reynolds found that the majority of CEOs think they could spend their time more effectively in at least a handful of places, while a significant minority feel that the bulk of their time could be spent more effectively. In a time-starved world where there are massive decisions on your plate every day, that's a huge problem.

Ask yourself how you would allocate your time if you had 100 percent control over your calendar. Start with your personal priorities. How often do you want to see friends and family? Be specific and separate time for your spouse, kids, parents, etc. How many days per week do you want to be at the gym or playing your favorite sport? Can you carve out time on the weekends to volunteer? Do you occasionally want to bring your kids along so you can model the importance of giving back?

Everyone has a different personal agenda they want to fulfill. When I began a recent calendar analysis, there were a few items that I prioritized. I wanted to...

- have lunch with my mom or stepdad once per week.
- drop my kids off at school every day.
- play tennis for an hour and a half three times per week.
- do pro bono work for a few hours every week.

After you schedule your most critical personal items, fill in your calendar with your top work priorities. How many hours per week should you…

- dedicate to strategic thinking?
- spend reading about your industry and other relevant business items?
- spend in the field talking to customers and employees?
- dedicate to meetings?
- devote to professional and personal growth by working with an executive coach?

When you're finished compiling the list of items and the time you want to spend working on them, ask your assistant to research the last six months of your calendar and compare the time spent *actually doing* these items versus the time you *want to* spend on them.

Apply the 80/20 rule to determine what can be trimmed from your actual calendar to allow for the prioritization you desire. Ask your assistant to take action steps to ensure your top priorities compose the majority of your calendar.

Top priorities can vary based on industry, leadership style, and your specific business. A few categories that are somewhat ubiquitous are detailed in the following subsections.

SET ASIDE PLENTY OF TIME FOR STRATEGIC THINKING

The same Russell Reynolds study also found that most CEOs don't spend enough time on activities with long-term strategic orientation. Have your assistant block off regular time for strategic thinking and be sure to never cross it off the calendar. It can be moved if an important client comes to town and can only meet with you during that time, but never eliminate it; instead, have your assistant move it to a different time during the week. This calendar space cannot be canceled, because it allows you to focus on big-picture growth potential like M&A, product lines, customer types, changes in customer preferences, markets/geographies, technology shifts, and current and future competitive threats.

This time can include reading articles/books and listening to podcasts helpful to your role. Warren Buffet says, "I just sit in my office and read all day." Specifically, he estimates he spends about 80 percent of his working day reading and thinking. A good executive coach will cull the libraries of information available for you and send you only the most pertinent and potentially game-changing ideas from articles, books, and podcasts.

Make your strategic thinking time as uninterruptible as possible. Like everything else, this idea has some limits. If a vital issue is on fire, you need to know about it. However, it's estimated that needless interruptions cost an average of just over six hours per day.[48] Making matters more difficult is that it takes approximately twenty-three minutes to refocus.[49] Make it clear to everybody that you're not to be disturbed when taking time for strategic thinking unless it is an emergency. Leave a sign on the door so people don't come in and out, causing you to lose your train of thought on great ideas and have to restart your mental processes.

Empathy is still a factor. If someone interrupts you for something that isn't crucial despite the sign on the door, calmly and professionally clarify the few types of issues that are justifiable for an interruption during this time. And do it one-on-one; not with other people present or in listening distance.

LEARN FROM THE FRONT LINE

Strategic thinking and discussions with board members are important to the big picture, but so is spending time in the field with all levels of your constituents, including employees, customers, and suppliers.

During my time on Wall Street, I closely followed Robert Tillman, Robert Niblock, and Robert Hull from the home improvement retailer Lowe's, and they were one of the most elite leadership teams I had ever studied. CEO Tillman was known for devoting a big chunk of his time with customers and team members. He would meet them in stores and have meals with them. Tillman would go out of his way to find out what they were seeing in the trenches and listen to their top ideas for improvement. Their "on the front lines" approach was a key contributor to Lowe's stock performing incredibly well under their leadership.

When I became a CEO coach many years later, a client running a large company asked me, "Where do you think I could add the most value in my business?" I told him to do an 80/20 analysis of his customers, including their current revenue and profitability contribution, as well as the potential for growth. This would help determine the most important customers to whom he—as the CEO—should dedicate more time.

I further advised him to find out what the most important goals were for his customers, the specific challenges that were preventing them from getting there, and how he could help them. More specifically, I told him to ask his customers how he could remove any friction or roadblocks they were experiencing in getting what they desire out of his product. If you take a similar approach, you'll have an enormous opportunity to prove your company as a trusted partner, which could especially help you pick up market share in an economic downturn.

ATTEND ONLY THE MOST URGENT MEETINGS

One way to make time for talking to customers and other stake-holders is by cutting down on the number of meetings you attend. The *Harvard Business Review* recently found that CEOs spend 72 percent of their time in meetings. Most leaders admitted that the vast majority of those meetings could be trimmed to thirty or even fifteen minutes.

Be stingier about meetings. For every invite you receive, determine if your attendance at the meeting is critical. Often, you'll be invited to meetings that address low-level concerns. Trust your people to take care of these matters and spend that time more effectively elsewhere. Enact a ruthless prioritization of attending only meetings that move the needle.

Whether you attend a meeting or not, the host should circulate a draft of the agenda that "trims the fat" and includes only the most important issues that must be addressed. That will allow your assistant or chief of staff to determine whether you should attend. Regardless of your presence, the host's agenda should also include proposed solutions so people can come to the meeting prepared. Meetings can now move along quickly because everyone arrives ready to debate the solutions and propose their own ideas. This can create more time on everyone's calendar.

To make meetings even more productive, establish a standard for when and how you'll meet with key team members individually for nonemergencies. Have the assistants block both calendars on the same day and time every week. Keep them short. With proper preparation, twenty minutes can be enough in most circumstances.

It is the team member's responsibility to keep a running list of the most vital issues throughout the week and prioritize what they absolutely need to discuss with you at the next meeting. Much like preparing an eighteen-minute TED talk, everyone will prioritize by using the 80/20 rule to trim the fat out of the agenda. They'll also learn to solve problems and make their own executive decisions on less important topics.

ESTABLISH AN EMAIL ROUTINE

Not attending routine meetings can open a lot of calendar space. Optimizing your email practices is another big productivity enhancer.

In a lot of ways, your assistant can be your gatekeeper. Aside from ensuring that annoying phone calls don't get through and preserving uninterrupted strategic thinking time, your assistant can also help manage your email to ensure you see only what's necessary. Have them unsubscribe you from noncritical lists and block any junk that ends up in your inbox.

Many team members are inclined to copy leaders on every email. It's understandable, as people might feel like they need to cover their tracks by ensuring everyone at the top knows what's going on in matters that are crucial to their jobs. If you create the culture of trust and candor we talked about earlier, much of that feeling will dissipate. To play it safe, tell everybody that you only want to be copied on the organization's most significant issues.

Silence notifications for your inbox or close out of it altogether so you can do deep, focused work. If you keep email notifications on, your mental focus will be distracted by a nonstop barrage of emails that aren't urgent. This is a substantial part of the interruptions that cost most people six hours per day. Instead, establish an email routine where you check your inbox once in the morning and once toward the end of the day. You can process your inbox in these two batches of time to get it back to zero.

As a hedge fund manager, I checked email once before the market opened and again just after it closed. I told my trader to text me if an emergency or anything earth-shattering happened. Except for a few family members and the head of our firm, that was the only text alert I kept unhidden during the day. That routine allowed me to perform deep work on stocks all day, where some others may have been distracted by real-time stock price movements and on-screen email notifications.

More recently, an executive coaching client who moved into more of a chairman role hired me to help the individual who replaced him as CEO. In his previous role, the new CEO was accustomed to constant interruptions. His daily routine included putting out many low-level fires. One of my most important jobs was to help him systematically remove himself from as many of those as possible, so he could focus on the big-picture items associated with his new role.

I advised the new CEO to have his assistant carve out time to work from home for strategic thinking before coming to the office. Then, I suggested that he schedule weekly twenty-minute meetings with each member of his C-suite where they would cover only the most crucial topics. I also advised him to ensure that he express his faith in their ability to handle the lower-level fires on their own. Lastly, I recommended that he establish standard policies on what qualified as an emergency worthy of interruption, while saving everything else important for the weekly meeting. I wanted him to clearly define what qualified as urgent and important—the upper-left corner of the Eisenhower Matrix.

TOTAL TIME SAVED

Imagine the possibilities of what you can do with all the time you'll save by employing the tactics in this chapter. There are many actionable takeaways that could add up to hours saved every day. Multiply that by the number of days in a week, month, and year, and you'll be amazed at how much your productivity soars. More importantly, think of the potential to scale your business and have more space for personal priorities with all that renewed time and energy at your disposal.

All the lessons provided to this point are crucial to leading without burnout. The next chapter, however, may be the most important of all—decision-making. Once you add that into the mix of everything else you've learned, deep personal and professional growth are inevitable.

LEAD WITHOUT BURNOUT

▶ Once you buy into the 80/20 rule, use the optimized Eisenhower Matrix to vastly improve productivity for you and your team.

▶ Religiously using snapshots will save tremendous time, prevent lost knowledge, and make your leadership and business run more efficiently.

▶ Ruthless prioritization of your calendar is key to optimizing time.

CHAPTER 8

DECISION-MAKING

"It is in your moments of decision that your destiny is shaped."

— Tony Robbins, American author
and motivational speaker

A n oft-cited statistic says that the average person makes about thirty-five thousand decisions per day. The word *average* indicates a middle ground, meaning some make far fewer decisions while others make many more. As a business leader, I'm certain that you fall into the category of "more." You may need to make decisions about who to hire, when to outsource, how to expand into new areas, and if an M&A is the right thing for your business. The list goes on. Additionally, your decisions often determine the fate of others—team members, customers, suppliers, etc. Few things are more important than growing the quality of your decision-making process to even higher levels.

Scores of studies show that decision-making should be swift and with conviction. Let's walk through some key skills—checklists, premortems, and mastery of cognitive biases—that will help you do that. Taking action on these items to improve the speed, certainty, and effectiveness of your decision-making process could be the most impactful lesson of all to lead without burnout.

"The way to maximize outcome is to concentrate on process."

—Seth Klarman, billionaire investor,
hedge fund manager, and author

CHECKLISTS

American surgeon, writer, and renowned public health expert Atul Gawande authored a book called *Checklist Manifesto*. In it, he emphasizes, "Under conditions of complexity, not only are checklists a help, but they are a requirement for success."

Gawande explains that surgeons and nurses using checklists in operating rooms for tasks, such as washing hands and making sure the correct part of the patient's body is marked for surgery, have reduced deaths by as much as 47 percent. A staggering figure, for sure.

So, checklists are a vital requirement for success in a complex endeavor such as surgery. Might you benefit from applying checklists to your complex task of making important business decisions? As Gawande goes on to say, "Even the most expert among us can gain from searching out the patterns of mistakes and failures and putting a few checks in place."

Mistakes are painful and expensive when they happen, but they can provide a form of ROI. There is tremendous value in learning from them so that the next time a similar situation occurs, you won't repeat the same form of failure. A problem exists, however, if the scenario happens years later. You might simply forget, or you could get caught up in the tidal wave of emotions of the current circumstances and fall victim to cognitive biases. As Reinhart and Rogoff showed in their famous book *This Time is Different*, leaders often make poor decisions when they fail to appreciate historical patterns.

Avoid relying on your memory or allowing emotions and cognitive biases to sweep you away by writing your top ten lessons learned from past mistakes. Include this business checklist as part of your cultural bylaws. For major decisions, have each team member who is involved go down the list and ask themselves, "If we go forward with this decision, would we be violating any of these lessons learned or repeating any of these previous mistakes?"

Arrange for a meeting with everyone involved in the decision. Discuss how the decision would fare on each of the ten lessons, checking them off one by one. Force yourselves to agree, no matter how tempting it may be, to not move forward with a decision that violates anything on the checklist, except under rare circumstances. The bar is extremely high for "this time is different." The final result will be a decision made with greater conviction that enables a much higher potential for success.

Keep a journal handy in your desk where you write any critical mistakes and/or lessons learned from the day. Evaluate whether any of them were significant enough to replace something on your top-ten checklist.

> *"No wise pilot, no matter how great his talent and experience, fails to use his checklist."*
>
> **— Charlie Munger, vice chairman of Berkshire Hathaway**

PREMORTEMS

Suppose a big decision is upcoming and you're open to using other tools to make the best possible choice. Conduct a premortem and plan for different precarious scenarios.

Picture yourself in the future, having failed in the situation at hand. What are the most likely reasons you failed? What steps can you take now to lower the odds those things happen? What adjustments will you make if those risks begin to emerge?

Optimism is a value many companies hold dear. There is a difference between optimism and blind faith or not performing comprehensive due diligence. Stay optimistic if it benefits you, but be wary of overconfidence, as it is one of the most common reasons for poor decision-making. Research from the consulting firm McKinsey shows that conducting premortems reduces overconfidence in teams more than any other form of risk analysis by a significant margin.[50]

> *"A project premortem is just as important as a post-mortem. Failing to do a premortem can ruin even well-thought-out strategies for long-term success. If we anticipate later actions that can undermine our plans, we can improve the likelihood of staying on course."*
>
> —Annie Duke, world champion poker
> player and author of *Thinking in Bets*

MY TECHNICAL FOUL

The most embarrassing moment of my professional life resulted from my failure to conduct a premortem. It occurred while I was exclusively volunteering and had no plans of returning to work anytime soon. However, an NBA owner asked me if I would present to his leadership on using analytics to improve an NBA team. My wife told me, "If you have interest in being an analytics advisor in the NBA one day, this might be your chance. I know you're not thinking of going back to work yet, but these types of opportunities aren't going to be around forever." As usual, that was smart advice my wife gave me.

I put together a slide deck to present to one of the team owners, the president, and GM. The GM asked to see how certain players ranked on total production using analytics. As I glanced at the Excel spreadsheet on my laptop, I felt my heart begin to pound rapidly through my chest. Then my mouth dried out and I had this bitter, metallic taste in my mouth as my anxiety soared. I noticed I had a surprise player ranked high in my data set, even ahead of Lebron James. It was not Steph Curry, Kevin Durant, or any other superhuman NBA All-Star. It was Landry Fields. Landry played five seasons for the Knicks and Raptors—an accomplishment that 99 percent of the world would not be capable of—but even Landry himself would admit that he was never on the same level, as a player, as Lebron James.

I love my Stanford alumni, but c'mon! As I saw the look of shock on the GM's face and heard him let out an awkward little laugh, I froze. Before I could come up with any explanation, the president accurately blurted out, "Well, that's horses*&t." He zipped on to one more question before quickly ending the discussion.

I had not conducted a premortem, which would have identified "a bug/error in the large data set" as a top reason I could fail in that meeting. That would have caused me to take action beyond simply scanning the data once. Our eyes miss big things all the time!

Much like engaging a proofreader for a book or essay, I would have had a second set of eyes review all my data. I also would have prepared a logical explanation in case both of our sets of eyes missed something that big. I learned the value of performing a premortem, cleaned the bugs in the data, and took these lessons with me the next time I met with an NBA team.

Before I met with the Pacers, I conducted a premortem and determined the most likely reasons for failure for which I should plan. What if I don't have my laptop directly in front of me when someone asks me about free agents or draft prospects? While I couldn't know the analytics of all two hundred free agents and 150 draft prospects without my laptop, I could dedicate significant time to memorizing my favorite ideas and the analytical reasons behind them for the Pacers, based on their needs and draft position.

I flew out to Indianapolis and met with the Pacers' GM and VP of ops. I had my laptop in front of me the entire time, though I was mentally exhausted after two and a half hours of questions. Then, I walked into the owner Herb Simon's office. He and other executives asked me an array of additional questions. After four straight hours of discussion, Herb said, "I want you to meet our president, Larry Bird. Just leave your stuff in my office. We'll come back to get it later."

Herb and I walked into Larry's office. Sure enough, Larry started asking me questions, and I didn't have my laptop. He asked me who my top unrestricted free agent backup centers were. I recalled my premortem preparation and provided an answer without hesitating. He followed up by asking which guys I had ranked highly who were expected to go late in the first round. I was able to answer that one with conviction as well. I had done a premortem, so I was ready.

This time, I was offered an advisory role by an NBA owner. Herb said that a key reason I stood out to him was my ability to provide detailed answers to questions from Larry on the spot. That positive result happened only because I pictured myself failing, identified several key reasons why, and took steps in advance so I could adapt in the moment. Where can you execute a similar process in your business?

GAME PREPARATION

Head coach Nate McMillan was a shining example of the power of premortems. He would think about the most likely reasons we could fail to beat an opponent. These would influence his approach and allow him to plan adjustments in advance. For example, before one of our games, I remember him talking about some of the scenarios he was exploring in preparation:

"What if they roll out this lineup with these four shooters surrounding their playmaker?"

"What if they run the pick and roll with these two players to create a size mismatch?"

He always had moves ready for various options that opponents could use. That way, the team could make a swift adjustment with conviction before the game got out of hand. It's just one of the many reasons he is considered an elite head coach.

WALL STREET EVENT PLANNING

I also used premortems in my Wall St. experience. For example, if I was coming into an earnings report for one of the stocks I owned, I would plan around the possibilities of that event going sideways.

If the company missed earnings expectations badly and the reasons they missed proved my investment thesis wrong, I would want to exit the investment. However, I needed to know how low the stock had to open for me to temporarily hold it, so I wouldn't end up selling at the same time as everyone else. Premortems were particularly important in this situation, because making an emotional reaction to "just get the hell out of the damned thing" no matter how far down the stock opened is almost always a mistake. The excessive selling pressure would often abate over the course of the day and I would get a better price to exit my failed investment.

But what if the company missed its earnings target due to temporary factors, and my long-term thesis remained intact? I needed to know what price was enticing enough for me to add to the position and how big I wanted to go with it. The last thing I wanted was to get scared away when the stock was selling off and I was feeling the real-time pressure. Preparing with a sizing model that assigned certain investment position sizes based on the price, upside potential, reward-to-risk ratio, and conviction score gave me a scientific approach that took out the emotions of reacting in the moment.

Premortems are pivotal to succeeding as a hedge fund investor. They can be even more impactful for you as a business leader.

LEADING WITH PREMORTEMS

Have you performed premortems to determine the most likely reasons you could fail to reach your business and growth goals? What steps can you take now to better protect yourself from your biggest competitive threats? If the macroeconomic environment pushes your revenues well below budget, you may need to cut expenses. Have you determined where those reductions will come from first? If the downward trend continues, where can you cut from next, while minimizing the harm to your longer-term growth outlook?

If you're making an acquisition, entering a new product line, or deciding on certain customers to prune, why might those initiatives fail? What can you do now, and what will you do if things start to turn south? Devote a strategic thinking session or two for each major initiative to perform premortems and plan for precarious scenarios. It's often this preparation that stimulates growth and sustains success.

> *"Steve Jobs saw that you can change the world through careful planning. Long-term planning is often undervalued by our indefinite short-term world."*
>
> —Peter Thiel, cofounder of PayPal, Palantir Technologies, and Founders Fund

MASTERING COGNITIVE BIASES

From my hedge fund management experience you just read about, you can see how emotions can wreak havoc on making consistently solid decisions. Minimizing the impact isn't as easy as it seems, however.

Don't underestimate the power of your own cognitive biases. To become an elite decision-maker, study the work done by the greats in this arena, including Dan Ariely, Robert Cialdini, and Daniel Kahneman. Their work shows how cognitive biases can ruin the decision-making of even the most brilliant people. Let's touch upon a handful.

COGNITIVE DISSONANCE AND CONFIRMATION BIAS

Let's use a hot-button political issue to dissect how your own predetermined thinking can affect decision-making. What is your stance on, say, government intervention in the economy? Imagine you recently read several articles from a respected bipartisan publication with strong, unbiased evidence that is overwhelmingly oppositional to your opinion. Would you lean more heavily into other articles that support your point of view, or would you honestly consider changing your opinion?

Most people like to think they're open-minded enough to change their opinion on any issue. The reality is quite the opposite. When presented with new information about a subject that contradicts your views, the inconsistencies create a mental toll called cognitive dissonance. Human nature dictates that you will largely discount it in favor of leaning even more heavily into your original argument. You may further this confirmation bias by searching for new articles and interpreting them in a biased way to confirm your original view. We all have these tendencies, but by becoming acutely aware of them and writing past examples of them in your lessons checklist, you can minimize their effects on the choices you make.

My most profound experience with cognitive dissonance and confirmation bias nearly ended my hedge fund career shortly after it started.

Ultimate Electronics (ULTE) had suffered through systems issues that were negatively impacting the customer experience in their stores. I felt this created an attractive valuation if they could stabilize the situation and start to turn it around, so I started to accumulate ULTE stock in my portfolio. Because the company had a large presence in the Midwest, I went to visit a lot of stores to find out for myself how things were playing out.

The first two stores I visited revealed continued problems in the customer experience. Product was difficult to locate. I compared prices with local Best Buy stores and found a much larger gap than expected. I wanted so badly to believe ULTE would turn things around that these findings created feelings of cognitive dissonance. I invented reasons why the customer experience was still challenging at these two stores but could be better elsewhere. As I visited more stores, my confirmation bias urged me to ask leading questions of customers like, "So, your shopping experience here is no longer a disaster, right?" I latched onto anything remotely positive I heard in their responses and discounted the negative comments.

I came back from my trip and did not sell the stock. In the ensuing weeks, ULTE's share price continued to bleed, culminating in an awful earnings report. I eventually sold the stock before the losses became even more career-threatening, but significant damage had been done.

In that situation, I had downplayed data that ran counter to my analysis of a stock. Instead of dispassionately evaluating it, I sought alternative explanations that would support what I wanted to believe. I wish I had been more self-aware of this cognitive dissonance and confirmation bias, especially by reviewing a past related mistake that landed on my lessons checklist. Then I would have conducted a more fact-based search for information and been more intellectually honest. I took a much bigger loss on ULTE than I should have. Have you made any business mistakes from doggedly clinging to pre-existing beliefs or underappreciating contradictory evidence? Have you ever yelled at the television that your team is losing largely because the referees are unfairly giving the other team all the calls, conveniently ignoring the close calls that went in your team's favor? We are all subject to this type of bias.

Write on your lessons checklist, and remind yourself repeatedly, that evidence-based intellectual honesty will always help you to be more successful than succumbing to your emotional biases. This is true in personal relationships as well as business. If you're like everybody else, you've had arguments with your significant other. You probably listened well in some of them, validating their point and truly allowing it to change your behavior. In others what you heard caused cognitive dissonance; you got defensive and cherry-picked interpretations that were favorable to you. Which approach has worked out better for you and your relationship?

> *"We think, each of us, that we're much more rational than we are. And we think that we make our decisions because we have good reasons to make them. Even when it's the other way around. We believe in the reasons because we've already made the decision."*
>
> —Daniel Kahneman

RESIST RECENCY BIAS

People tend to believe what they want to believe. They also tend to most vividly remember and overvalue the most recent events they've witnessed. This is called recency bias, and a great example of it exists in professional sports.

Sometimes you see a mid-level role player on a professional sports team catch fire during a playoff run and turn that elite performance into a massive four-to-five-year contract. Most of the time we see that same player revert to their prior mid-level performance for the rest of their career.

Recency bias makes you believe that the four-hundred-minute sample size of superior performance you just witnessed is going to become the norm, rather than the ten-thousand-minute sample size you saw before.

Recency bias exists everywhere. The *Harvard Business Review* estimates that 70 to 90 percent of mergers and acquisitions fail. Although many reasons exist for this unsettling data, an underappreciated one is related to recency bias. These transactions often happen at peak profit margins and peak valuation multiples.

Buyers extrapolate the target company's recent profit margins, underappreciating how far along in the industry or business cycle the company is at the time of the M&A. When you're near the top of an industry or business cycle, valuations also become very elevated. Paying recent multiples gets justified by fear of missing out. If you find yourself in this situation, be aware of how recency bias may be influencing your thought process. Determine the other company's normalized profitability across an entire cycle. Be disciplined in establishing the maximum valuation you're willing to pay that gives you a strong ROI.

These recency bias situations can also play to your advantage in reverse. Some of my highest return investments as a hedge fund manager came when I bought a heavy portion of a stock that was under pressure due to recent temporary factors. Dick's Sporting Goods sometimes reported a slow season largely due to inclement weather patterns in the Northeast. Subsequently, recency bias drove their stock price down. That was a great opportunity to buy an exceptionally-run business with an excellent long-term growth outlook. Looking three to five years out, I could appreciate those short-term issues were going to disappear and be a nonfactor.

Similarly, if you avoid a bidding war today, your balance sheet will be a competitive advantage in a cycle downturn. In that scenario, others may not have the risk appetite or balance sheet flexibility to compete for acquisitions. They may be swayed by recency bias, extrapolate trough margins, and not drive up your price for acquisitions.

Being cognizant of how recency bias works both ways may help you capitalize on your version of Dick's Sporting Goods—a dream acquisition at an attractive price—when the timing is right.

> *"The one real edge you can have as an investor is a behavioral advantage. For us [at Lux Capital] that means having a longer time horizon than the average investor. We call this time arbitrage. If the average investor is looking for a signal of success in a year or two—and we are looking at something that might not give us a signal for four or five years—then by definition there will be fewer investors looking to fund what we are funding."*
>
> —Josh Wolfe, cofounder of Lux Capital

BEWARE OF THE SUNK COST FALLACY

It's easy to get caught up in the past. You want value for the time and money you've invested, which means you're often hesitant to "cut the cord" with a failing venture. Sticking with a mistake solely because you feel you've already invested too much to back out is the sunk cost fallacy.

When you're deciding what to do about a struggling initiative, employee, or something similar, ask yourself, if you had the chance for a fresh start on the decision today, would you still do it? Would you still invest in the initiative or hire the employee? If not, don't dwell on the costs you've already incurred. If it seems unlikely that the situation will turn around and provide a real upside, strongly consider cutting the cord. How much is this situation distracting your focus and weighing on your time, money, or mental energy? How will you feel if you shed its weight?

In my early investing years, I fell victim to this mistake several times. For example, let's say I bought a stock and uncovered data points several months later that went against my investment thesis. At this point, the stock was down 10 percent from where I bought it. I might have thought, "I've already lost 10 percent, and there is a chance I could get back to even. If I can just recoup that loss, then, I'll walk away." Have you ever felt that way at a casino? That was the sunk cost fallacy interfering with my decision-making. Instead of thinking about what I had already invested and lost, I should have evaluated the merits of that stock every day at its going rate.

LIMIT GROUPTHINK

Suppose you have an upcoming big decision to make, like whether to enter a new market. Don't simply open up the floor for thoughts. Instead, have team members separately rate a short list of important variables, submit them to you, and keep their opinions private from others until the group discussion. This limits groupthink, where the tendency to conform to others can lead to suboptimal decision-making.

Groupthink can allow the most extroverted person in the group to pound the table against the new market and influence others to downplay their favorable evidence. Other times, the person who is most incentivized by entering the new market speaks buoyantly for it, causing others to become hesitant to speak against what benefits that person. By gathering and reviewing the ratings in advance, you can lead a more balanced and intellectually honest discussion.

Give people a brief period after the group discussion to process everything that was said. Then, ask if they want to adjust any of their initial ratings based on the discussion. If so, they must write a brief explanation about why their opinion has changed. You will get more intellectually honest answers by using these processes. When reviewing the explanations, you'll recognize what is groupthink versus compelling evidence from the discussion.

Apply appropriate weights to everyone's ratings of that short list of variables and determine a score for the new market. Of course, that score isn't the final say in whether to move forward. However, quantifying the pros and cons of something like a new market with everyone's input can be quite powerful. It gives you a more scientific tool for higher-quality decision-making while limiting groupthink.

LEAVE THE OFFICE

When a big decision is coming up, your inclination might be to stay in the office until you're certain of your choice. However, despite your efforts to make the office as welcoming and comfortable as possible, it can still be associated with stress and anxiety. The office can also be a place of constant disruption with people trying to grab your attention, the phone ringing, and a constant influx of brush fires to extinguish. Does that really provide you with the distraction-free environment you need to make such an important decision—one you have researched for weeks that could have a significant impact on profitability? Remember a statistic we cited earlier, that it takes twenty-three minutes to refocus after an interruption.

Instead of locking yourself down, get out. Grab your laptop with all your snapshots and other notes on it, leave your phone behind, and go to a park or another quiet setting where you can think clearly. Getting this extra bit of space and open air can be exactly what you need to clear your head and avoid making an emotional decision.

"The best thinking has been done in solitude. The worst has been done in turmoil."

—Thomas Edison, American
inventor and businessperson

Whenever I made a big decision on a stock, I went to a specific spot in Central Park. Sometimes, I had been gathering information for weeks, but was unable to make a move until I could synthesize it all in that peaceful setting. I brought my snapshots of the potential investment and my checklist of mistakes with me. I sat there in my own headspace until I came to a decision about which I felt confident.

ELEVATE EVERYONE'S DECISION-MAKING

Ensure your teammates learn all the concepts mentioned in this chapter—checklists, premortems, and mastery of cognitive biases—to help everyone make swift, evidence-based decisions with conviction.

Few things are more impactful than enhancing your teammates' and your own decision-making processes. Imagine the reduced stress and burnout, increased growth and profitability, and improvements to work-life balance from making higher-quality decisions.

LEAD WITHOUT BURNOUT

▶ Using a checklist of lessons from past mistakes can slash the number of decisions that lead to bad outcomes.

▶ Premortems and planning for different scenarios raise your odds of success.

▶ Cognitive biases ruin the decisions of even the most brilliant people. Master these.

CONCLUSION

"Time is really the only capital that any human being has, and the only thing he can't afford to lose."

– Thomas Edison, American inventor and businessperson

N ow, for the most exciting part—taking action on everything you've learned to lead without burnout!

Hopefully, you took good notes while you were reading. Knowledge is great, but as we mentioned earlier, it doesn't help much unless you have a way to store it, access it, and apply it to the right situation when necessary.

When you're done reading, your first step toward leading without burnout is to block ninety minutes off this weekend's calendar to go through your notes and create a brief snapshot for each chapter. The following is a quick list of key takeaways on which you can focus your snapshots.

Chapter 1 demonstrated how true self-actualization stems from flourishing in many aspects of life, not just the professional. It's impossible to be the best at everything. Use the "vision and values" exercise to find out what matters most to you and take action to achieve greatness in those aspects of life. Use the Wheel of Life exercise to rate where you are now in those areas and where you want to be.

Chapter 2 explained the ineffectiveness of traditional mission statements and company values. Instead, you learned how to create cultural bylaws that will help attract and retain "A" players—perhaps the most critical part of leading without burnout. Execute the actionable steps in Chapter 2 to ensure your team members follow through on your newly created cultural bylaws.

Chapter 3 was about establishing a culture of two-way trust that frees up your time for strategic thinking, gives your team members greater purpose, and enhances talent retention.

Chapter 4 discussed the importance of implementing high candor in your culture to improve learning, decision quality, and employee engagement. Focus on setting the tone for curiosity and candor, asking open-ended questions, and empowering everyone to give positive and negative feedback to their team members and you. The feedback should be something everyone listens intently to and takes action to remedy. Actually listening is key here. When someone is speaking, the other party should be focused on their words, not thinking of their rebuttal.

Chapter 5 discussed the numerous ways of making mental health the top priority in your culture. Not only does it enhance loyalty, but it's also the right thing to do. Focus on care, empathy, recognition, gratitude, and demeanor. Imagine the possibilities if every organization took action on this snapshot alone. What would society look like if all companies made overall well-being their number-one cultural goal?

Chapter 6 gave you the step-by-step process to conduct the massive due diligence necessary to land "A" players that will radically improve your quality of life and allow you to scale your business faster and more effectively.

Chapter 7 outlined the top strategies needed to optimize your time and productivity, including the 80/20 Principle, an enhanced Eisenhower Matrix, snapshots, and ruthless calendar prioritization.

Chapter 8 focused on improving decision-making through checklists, premortems, and mastery of cognitive biases. To lead without burnout, you will need to put all the previously learned tools to the test to make high-quality decisions.

Once your snapshots are safely stored in the cloud, it's go time. Create a game plan of the key changes you're going to make and put those action steps on your to-do list and/or your calendar.

Every leader and organization is different. You may already have a culture of trust, but perhaps aspects of mental health could use a boost. You might already have good time optimization techniques, but you may need to work on prioritizing your calendar. Have snapshots available for all of the lessons learned in this book and choose the ones you need to work on now. In a few years, you might need to access different snapshots to solve new and emerging problems. Either way, you'll be equipped for a constantly changing business landscape. Most importantly, you'll be able to lead your company through it all without burning out yourself or those around you.

I challenge you to destroy any perceived limitations that may have formed in your mind based on what your peers are doing or experiencing. Use the tools and action steps in this book to choose, create, and execute *your* desired path for fulfillment. With these snapshots readily available—now and in the future—you'll be able to create more time for strategic thinking, strengthening family relationships, or for anything else you want to do. You can optimize your work-life relationship and overall well-being, the job satisfaction of your team members, and the growth of your business to achieve leadership transcendence.

How will you spend your newfound time? Just imagine the possibilities: they're limitless. Actually, don't *just imagine* anything. Make it happen!

CONTACT ME

Don't hesitate to reach out if I can be helpful to you, or if you want to share how your new path is working for you. My email is Ryan@TheStretchFive.com.

I'm considering holding an intimate in-person summit for CEOs and other business leaders where we dive deeper into some of the topics presented in this book. If you're interested, you can visit TheStretchFive.com/Summit.

NOTES

1 Jen Fisher, Steve Hatfield, and Paul H. Silvergate, "The C-Suite's Role in Well-Being," https://www2.deloitte.com/us/en/insights/topics/leadership/employee-wellness-in-the-corporate-workplace.html, June 22, 2022.

2 Matthew A. Killingsworth, "Experienced Well-Being Rises with Income, Even Above $75,000 per Year," https://www.pnas.org/doi/10.1073/pnas.2016976118, January 18, 2021.

3 Daniel Gross, "Why Aren't Successful People Happier?" *Strategy+Business*, September 26, 2019. https://www.strategy-business.com/article/Why-arent-successful-people-happier?utm_source=itw&utm_medium=NL20230502&utm_campaign=resp.

4 Val Matta, "Do Your Employees Know Your Mission Statement? This Is Why It's Important," https://careershift.com/blog/2016/08/do-employees-know-your-mission-statement/, August 29, 2016.

5 Juliana Lina, "Most Employees Don't Know Their Company's Corporate Values," https://www.fond.co/blog/new-data-company-core-values/, April 11, 2018.

6 Adam Robinson, "New Gallup Data Finds Only 1 in 4 Employees Believe in Their Company Values. This Strategy Can Change That," https://www.inc.com/adam-robinson/new-gallup-data-finds-only-1-in-4-employees-believe-in-their-company-values-this-strategy-can-change-that.html, May 29, 2019.

7 Charles Sull, Donald Sull, and Stefano Turconi, "When It Comes to Culture, Does Your Company Walk the Talk?" https://sloanreview.mit.edu/article/when-it-comes-to-culture-does-your-company-walk-the-talk/, July 21, 2020.

8 Anders BE Eklund, "63% of Employees Don't Have a Clear Understanding of the Company Vision — Here's Why!" https://www.linkedin.com/pulse/63-employees-dont-have-clear-understanding-company-vision-eklund/, November 2, 2017.

9 Sophie Kiderlin, "Overwhelming Majority of Gen Z Workers Would Quit Their Jobs over Company Values, LinkedIn Data Says," https://www.cnbc.com/2023/04/20/majority-of-gen-z-would-quit-their-jobs-over-company-values-linkedin.html, April 20, 2023.

10 Robert Kabakoff, "Develop Strategic Thinkers Throughout Your Organization," https://hbr.org/2014/02/develop-strategic-thinkers-throughout-your-organization, February 7, 2014.

11 Richard Horwath, "The Strategic Thinking Manifesto," https://www.strategyskills.com/pdf/The-Strategic-Thinking-Manifesto.pdf.

12 Karen Twaronite, "A Global Survey on the Ambiguous State of Employee Trust," https://hbr.org/2016/07/a-global-survey-on-the-ambiguous-state-of-employee-trust, July 22, 2016.

13 Grzegorz Szumski and Maciej Karwowski, "Exploring the Pygmalion Effect: The Role of Teacher Expectations, Academic Self-Concept, and Class Context in Students' Math Achievement," https://www.sciencedirect.com/science/article/abs/pii/S0361476X18300729?via%3Dihub, October, 2019.

14 Spencer Harrison, Erin Pinkus, and Jon Cohen, "Research: 83% of Executives Say They Encourage Curiosity. Just 52% of Employees Agree," https://hbr.org/2018/09/research-83-of-executives-say-they-encourage-curiosity-just-52-of-employees-agree, September 20, 2018.

15 Chris Bradley, Martin Hirt, and Sven Smit, *Strategy Beyond the Hockey Stick: People, Probabilities, and Big Moves to Beat the Odds* (Hoboken, New Jersey: John Wiley & Sons, February 6, 2018).

16 Jack Zenger and Joseph Folkman, "Overcoming Feedback Phobia: Take the First Step," https://hbr.org/2013/12/overcoming-feedback-phobia-take-the-first-step, December 16, 2013.

17 "Mental Disorders." World Health Organization. Accessed April 26, 2023. https://www.who.int/news-room/fact-sheets/detail/mental-disorders.

18 Claudia Elsig, "The Truth about the Mental Health of CEOs." The CALDA Clinic, November 19, 2022. https://caldaclinic.com/the-truth-about-the-mental-health-of-ceos/.

19 Brie Weiler Reynolds, "FlexJobs Mental Health America Survey: Mental Health in the Workplace." *FlexJobs Job Search Tips and Blog* (blog), December 5, 2022. https://www.flexjobs.com/blog/post/flexjobs-mha-mental-health-workplace-pandemic/.

20 Kathryn Mayer, "Number of the Day: Mental Health Retention Risks." *HR Executive*, December 7, 2021. https://hrexecutive.com/hres-number-of-the-day-mental-health-retention-risks/.

21 "Shifting Tides: Changing Attitudes About Mental Health Care and the Workplace," n.d. https://join.modernhealth.com/future-of-mental-health-2021-report-forrester.html?utm_source=blog&utm_medium=article&utm_campaign=od_summary_blog.

22 Mindsharepartners, "2021 Mental Health at Work Report by Mind Share Partners," n.d. https://www.mindsharepartners.org/mentalhealthatworkreport-2021.

23 Ira Boudway, "The Five Pillars of Popovich." *Bloomberg.Com*, January 10, 2018. https://www.bloomberg.com/news/features/2018-01-10/the-five-pillars-of-gregg-popovich#xj4y7vzkg.

24 EY. "New EY Consulting Survey Confirms 90% of US Workers Believe Empathetic Leadership Leads to Higher Job Satisfaction and 79% Agree It Decreases Employee Turnover." *Cision PR Newswire*, October 14, 2021. https://www.prnewswire.com/news-releases/new-ey-consulting-survey-confirms-90-of-us-workers-believe-empathetic-leadership-leads-to-higher-job-satisfaction-and-79-agree-it-decreases-employee-turnover-301397246.html.

25 Mark C. Perna, "Gratitude Research Reveals Why Saying 'Thank You' Can Help Win the Talent War." *Forbes*, November 22, 2021. https://www.forbes.com/sites/markcperna/2021/11/22/gratitude-research-reveals-why-saying-thank-you-can-help-win-the-talent-war/?sh=5da0360fec74.

26 Kim Cameron, Carlos Mora, Trevor Leutscher, and Margaret Calarco, "Effects of Positive Practices on Organizational Effectiveness," Center for Positive Organizational Scholarship Ross School of Business University of Michigan.

27 Emily Kaplan, "The Power of Positive Coaching and Its Impact on the Stanley Cup Playoffs," *ESPN.com*, May 24, 2023. https://www.espn.com/nhl/story/_/id/37706646/power-positive-coaching-florida-panthers-paul-maurice-stanley-cup-playoffs.

28 Bravo Wellness, "Do Wellness Programs Save Companies Money?" *Bravo Wellness* (blog), July 21, 2021. https://www.bravowell.com/resources/do-wellness-programs-save-companies-money.

29 "PATH Health Consultants," n.d. http://www.pathhealthllc.com/about-us/about-path.htm.

30 Cathy McCullough, "The ROI of Business Coaching: Executive Coaching ROI Statistics (2023 Updated)," *Rhythm Systems* (blog), February 22, 2023. https://www.rhythmsystems.com/blog/the-roi-of-executive-coaching.

31 McKinsey & Company, "Americans Are Embracing Flexible Work—and They Want More of It," June 23, 2022. https://www.mckinsey.com/industries/real-estate/our-insights/americans-are-embracing-flexible-work-and-they-want-more-of-it.

32 Randstad and Randstad, "Randstad," *www.Randstad.com*, n.d. https://www.randstad.com/workforce-insights/hr-trends/flexibility-what-it-means-to-non-office-workers/.

33 Shengmin Liu, Huanhuan Xin, Li Shen, Jianjia He, and Jingfang Liu, "The Influence of Individual and Team Mindfulness on Work Engagement," *Frontiers in Psychology*, https://www.frontiersin.org/articles/10.3389/fpsyg.2019.02928/full, January 21, 2020.

34 Suzanne Taylor, "Employee Productivity: Mindfulness Could Increase Focus And Enable Better Collaboration," *Forbes*, April 22, 2021. https://www.forbes.com/sites/forbestechcouncil/2021/04/22/employee-productivity-mindfulness-could-increase-focus-and-enable-better-collaboration/?sh=75e5aa6dbae9.

35 Siu-kuen Azor Hui, PhD, MSPH, and Michael A. Grandner, PhD, MTR, "Trouble Sleeping Associated with Lower Work Performance and Greater Healthcare Costs: Longitudinal Data from Kansas State Employee Wellness Program," National Library of Medicine, https://www.ncbi.nlm.nih.gov/pmc/articles/PMC4610176/, October 2015.

36 Ron Friedman, "Regular Exercise Is Part of Your Job," *Harvard Business Review*, November 5, 2014. https://hbr.org/2014/10/regular-exercise-is-part-of-your-job.

37 Fran Maxwell, "Talent Strategy Is Company Strategy," *ChiefExecutive.Net*, April 12, 2023. https://chiefexecutive.net/talent-strategy-is-company-strategy/.

38 Steve Bates, "Majority of New Hires Say Job Is Not What They Expected," *SHRM*, April 10, 2018. https://www.shrm.org/resourcesandtools/hr-topics/employee-relations/pages/newhiresfeelmisled.aspx.

39 Robert Half Talent Solutions, "Nine in 10 New Hires Would Leave a Job That Fails to Meet Expectations within the First Month," https://www.roberthalf.co.uk/press/nine-10-new-hires-would-leave-job-fails-meet-expectations-within-first-month, April 8, 2020.

40 Andrew Chamberlain, "Why Interview Sources Matter in Hiring: Exploring Glassdoor Interviews Data - Glassdoor," *Glassdoor Economic Research*, August 12, 2015. https://www.glassdoor.com/research/interview-sources/.

41 William Arruda, "Why Your Company's People Are The Best Recruiters And How To Engage Them In Hiring," *Forbes*, October 31, 2022. https://www.forbes.com/sites/williamarruda/2022/10/31/why-your-companys-people-are-the-best-recruiters-and-how-to-engage-them-in-hiring/?sh=1fdf9a963ec9&utm_source=newsletter&utm_medium=email&utm_campaign=dailydozen&utm_content=uaddsubscribe&cdlcid=62b9fd3ff9c34d1310064a96.

42 Seamus Roddy, "5 Employee Referral Program Strategies to Hire Top Talent," *HR Clutch Report*, April 22, 2020. https://clutch.co/hr/resources/5-employee-referral-program-strategies-hire-top-talent.

43 "New Survey: Performative Work and Productivity Theater | Visier." n.d. https://www.visier.com/blog/productivity-survey-shows-performative-work/.

44 Julia Gifford, "The Rule of 52 and 17: It's Random, But It Ups Your Productivity," *The Muse*, June 2020. https://www.themuse.com/advice/the-rule-of-52-and-17-its-random-but-it-ups-your-productivity.

45 "Sitting Risks: How Harmful Is Too Much Sitting?" Mayo Clinic. July 13, 2022. https://www.mayoclinic.org/healthy-lifestyle/adult-health/expert-answers/sitting/faq-20058005.

46 Renée Onque, "Taking 10,000 Steps a Day Can Help You Live Longer, but How Fast You Go Matters, New Study Shows," *CNBC*, October 28, 2022. https://www.cnbc.com/2022/10/27/new-study-on-benefits-of-walking-frequency-speed-and-how-many-steps.html.

47 Luis Rivera, "Ecopsychology: How Immersion in Nature Benefits Your Health," *Yale Environment 360*, January 9, 2020. https://e360.yale.edu/features/ecopsychology-how-immersion-in-nature-benefits-your-health.

48 Brigid Schulte, "Work Interruptions Can Cost You 6 Hours a Day. An Efficiency Expert Explains How to Avoid Them," *Washington Post*, June 1, 2015. https://www.washingtonpost.com/news/inspired-life/wp/2015/06/01/interruptions-at-work-can-cost-you-up-to-6-hours-a-day-heres-how-to-avoid-them/.

49 Mark Gloria, Mary Czerwinski, and Shamsi T. Iqbal, "Effects of Individual Differences in Blocking Workplace Distractions," *CHI*, April 21-26, 2018.

50 "Bias Busters: Premortems: Being Smart at the Start," McKinsey & Company, April 3, 2019. https://www.mckinsey.com/capabilities/strategy-and-corporate-finance/our-insights/bias-busters-premortems-being-smart-at-the-start.

ACKNOWLEDGEMENTS

My first few attempts to write this section were futile. I initially had hundreds of people I wanted to acknowledge and thank. I found it preposterous to try to whittle it down or leave anyone out. So, have we crossed paths in this life, including but not limited to Sacramento, Stanford, NYC, Wall Street, the consumer sector, investing, volunteering, the NBA, Minor League Baseball, the MLS, executive coaching, or the production of this book? Then almost assuredly I have learned from you, been inspired by you, and felt supported by you. I owe you thanks for the impact you've had on my life.

ABOUT THE AUTHOR

R yan Renteria is a CEO coach, diverse board director, and
speaker who helps leaders optimize professional and personal growth. He spent nine years at Goldman Sachs and
large hedge funds. Ryan became a partner and managing director
of consumer investments at age twenty-five and, after strong returns, left Wall Street at thirty for charitable pursuits. He spent
nine years as an analytics advisor to Indiana Pacers coaches and executives. Ryan was part of the ownership group of the Milwaukee
Brewers' AA Minor League Baseball team and a potential MLS
team. He earned a BA from Stanford University. Learn more at
TheStretchFive.com.